THE BIRTH OF THE
ROUTEMASTER

John Aldridge
Ken Blacker
Gavin Booth
Stewart J Brown
Ken Glazier
Alan A Townsin
James Whiting

Capital Transport

Introduction

Between May and August 1954 the first prototype of London's Routemaster fleet was built. Fifty years later, in a very different world, Routemasters were still providing excellent service in London, and elsewhere in the case of sold examples. This book was conceived as one of the celebrations of the type's fiftieth anniversary. Concentrating on the early history of the RM's development, the book makes much use of new research: around 95% of the information has not previously been published.

Thanks for assistance with this work must first go to Philip Wood and Beth Polack at the Transport for London archives, who on numerous visits located from the vaults below 55 Broadway the files needed for the story. Thanks are also extended to Tony Beard, Charles Greystock, John Lewis, Andrew Morgan, Hugh Robertson and Bob Williamson, and in particular to Colin Curtis for his help with photographs and information, and to the late Michael Robbins.

The contributors to this book will be known to most readers. Ken Blacker has written the definitive two-volume history of the Routemaster, Alan Townsin was a draughtsman at AEC when the Routemaster was being designed and has written many books on bus subjects, Ken Glazier has written more historical books about London buses than anyone else, John Aldridge, Gavin Booth and Stewart Brown have spent many years in the fields of transport journalism and historical research on buses. A better team of contributors to this book one could not wish for.

James Whiting

First published 2004
Second printing 2007

ISBN 978-1-85414-280-1

Published by Capital Transport Publishing
P.O. Box 250, Harrow, HA3 5ZH

Printed by Thomson Press, Lyon Road, Harrow, HA1 2AF

Contents

A New Bus for London

The labour market had been considerably changed by the Second World War, leading to drives for productivity in manufacturing and service industries. Two separate strands of enquiry, first into new methods of bus building and second into higher capacity buses, came together in the design of the Routemaster.

On 24th September 1946, before any post-war RTs had entered service, the London Passenger Transport Board's Chief Mechanical Engineer A A M Durrant wrote a memo to its Chairman Lord Ashfield requesting £2,500 for preliminary development work on the design of a "four-wheel vehicle of chassisless construction embodying substantial improvements in springing, engine mounting and general passenger amenities" as a successor to the RT. On 31st July 1947, the Deputy General Manager of London Transport's road services submitted a memo about a new chassisless double-deck bus to be built using light alloy materials. The memo began by stating that this was where the future development of bus design would be directed. The advantages of this method of bus building were given as the lighter weight that would result and improved methods of construction that would reduce the amount of skilled labour required in manufacture. This memo sought permission to proceed with the design and construction of 25 chassisless light alloy buses as part of the order placed by London Transport with Leyland Motors Ltd earlier in the year for 500 8ft wide buses. The proposal was that there would be 475 RTWs of standard construction and 25 buses of the lightweight construction.

A memo dated 9th July 1947 and from the same officer had spoken of the construction by Beadle & Company of Dartford of four experimental single-deck buses of chassisless design using aluminium for the bodies, "this being a complete departure from previous practice". Although aluminium had been used for bus bodies in a few earlier designs and chassisless construction had been used on some of London Transport's trolleybuses built in 1939 and 1940, Beadle was the first company to combine the two developments in the UK. The Beadle vehicles had been inspected by London Transport engineers and the company had been asked to submit a design to the Board for the construction of a double decker embodying the same principles as their single-deck vehicles.

On 4th September, the proposal for 25 chassisless lightweight double deckers went to the Board for approval, this time naming both AEC and Leyland as potential suppliers of the running units for the buses. No decision appears to have been made prior to the transfer of responsibility for London Transport to the British Transport Commission on 1st January 1948 and the idea for 25 experimental buses fell by the wayside.

In 1949, two separate proposals were looked at for buses of higher capacity than those currently running in London. First there was a proposal for a 30ft long two-axle double decker seating 70 passengers and second a proposal for a 32ft 6ins long single decker seating 30 passengers with space for 36 standing. Both proposals exceeded the then current maximum lengths permitted. The 70-seater bus was a revival of a similar idea of ten years earlier. One of the options being considered shortly before the start of the Second World War had been the use of the 70-seater buses, instead of trolleybuses, to replace trams on the routes in south London.

The standee single decker proposal was put forward by Mr F A A Menzler, London Transport's Chief Development and Research Officer following "a suggestion recently advocated in the technical press". He suggested that such a vehicle could be considered for urban short-distance services and that the proportion of seated to standing passengers could be increased for longer-distance operations. The bus would be built using light alloys.

The main obstacle to high capacity buses was seen to be fare collection. In 1949 the standard means of ticket issue was by the Bell Punch system, whereby individual pre-printed tickets were carried in a rack and validated in a ringing punch machine on issue. Mechanisation of ticket issue was still limited and it was accepted that mechanisation of ticketing and simplification of fares were means of enabling higher capacity buses to be introduced. One of the arguments for single-deck high-capacity buses as opposed to double deckers was that the conductor could get around quicker and keep a better eye on passengers if he had only one deck to look after. At no time was one-man operation of these buses considered. The layout of a standee single decker would need to include a clear gangway along which the conductor could pass to collect fares. Separate entrance and exit was recommended to speed up boarding and alighting; there was no mention of doors, which were prohibited on buses by Metropolitan Police regulations at the time. The engine would be mounted under the floor to give maximum space for passengers. Menzler was of the view that the balance of advantage lay with the single-deck option.

A A M Durrant, later to become known as the father of the Routemaster, responded in a memo dated 4th October 1949. He was far from impressed by the argument for a high-capacity single decker, pointing out that a vehicle with such a high proportion of standee accommodation was unlikely to be tolerated by the travelling public on the longer distance routes in the Central Area. He also felt that it was "a little optimistic" to believe that it would be possible to maintain a clear gangway to give free movement to the conductor. Furthermore it was "extremely unlikely" that, even if the Ministry were to permit 32ft 6ins long single deckers, the Metropolitan Police would approve their operation anywhere in its area.

Meanwhile a '70-Seater Bus Committee', chaired by Michael Robbins, was looking at the savings that could be made by introducing 70-seater double-deck buses. A draft report was completed in December 1949. The capital cost of the 70-seater bus was based on the assumption that the vehicle structure would be designed on a similar basis to the RT and that RT production methods would be used.

Among those on the committee was Peter Ongley, not long after to become involved in the development of the RM. The report assumed that the cost of a 70-seater double decker would be 11% greater than an RT, allowing for the additional tooling that would be necessary. No mention is made in the report of the possibility of a chassisless lightweight design – pointing out that the chassis would be "necessarily of a different type" (compared with the RT). The continued use of RT components, e.g. windows and seats, was assumed and so the body would virtually have been a 30ft long version of the RT or, more likely, RTW. Adding a standard sized window bay to the RT design would produce a bus 29ft 9½ins long.

In terms of depot and garage space, the replacement of 30ft long 70-seater trolleybuses by buses of the same length and passenger capacity clearly had no implications. If 70-seater buses were to replace the remaining trams in place of the scheduled 56-seaters the total number of buses needed could reduce.

At a meeting on 10th January 1950, figures in the region of 3,000 vehicles were being spoken of in relation to the 70-seater bus for tram and trolleybus replacement and selected existing bus routes. Durrant had been continuing his separate line of investigation into a chassisless bus for RT replacement and reported that an efficient and economical bus with 60 or 62 seats and with a length of 27 or 28 feet could be produced at the same cost and with similar manoeuvrability to the RT.

Brian Harbour, the Country Bus Operating Manager, said that the proposal should be seriously examined as an increase of four passengers would not hinder the conductor's efficiency and would provide some insurance against a future withdrawal of standing passengers. Although estimates for reductions in the numbers of buses needed with a 70-seater bus compared with one seating 56 like the RT ranged from 12% to 22%. F A A Menzler voiced concerns about the idea. A 70-seater, he felt, would result in a claim from the union for enhanced pay or even a second conductor and the anticipated financial gains would be partially, if not completely, offset by such a claim being met. He agreed with Brian Harbour that a detailed study of the 60-seater should proceed. The previous year, AEC had tried to interest London Transport in what AEC saw as the successor to the RT – the Regent IV. This design seated 60 passengers in a fully-fronted underfloor-engined double decker 27ft long, but Durrant was not keen on the seat spacing and felt in addition that the direction for future London double deckers pointed away from underfloor engines.

Ideas of a 70-seater bus were finally killed off in 1951 when Durrant and his team were asked to work on a 64-seater bus design of integral lightweight construction, if possible within the existing maximum permitted length of 27ft. From now on the vehicle that would succeed the RT and the vehicle for trolleybus replacement would be one and the same in the design that would become the Routemaster.

Durrant was a man of detail and on 18th December 1951, he sent a note headed 'The Bus of the Future' to London Transport's Chief Public Relations Officer David McKenna asking for details of comments that had been made on the subject of bus design in correspondence from members of the public. The response pointed out that very many suggestions had been made, "many of them of little or no merit – old stagers like the coloured light system for indicating vacant seats on the top deck".

Five areas were felt by the CPRO to be worth considering and his reply seems to be a mixture of public suggestions and some of his own pet ideas. On the matter of bell pushes, more were felt to be needed on the top deck so that passengers could ring before reaching the top of the stairs. The display of traffic notices was in need of review, the side windows being considered unsatisfactory and bodywork panels being liable to scratching if notices are posted on the paintwork. A properly designed panel was needed that would withstand the activities of the bill posters. A shallow recess was suggested above the rear wheel arch on the nearside, or the upright panel between the platform and the side windows. A box inside the bus for publicity leaflets and maps was also suggested. The 'To and from' boards carried in brackets along the bottom edge of the front downstairs passenger window to indicate places of interest the bus was passing were felt to be unsatisfactory. A simple mechanical device, a sliding screen or shutter, that would block out or remove the information once the bus had passed the place in question was suggested, to be operated by a switch in the driver's cab.

None of the above four suggestions was carried through to the final design. The fifth suggestion was for a used ticket box to be fitted at the top of the stairs as well as on the platform. "The space on the offside just behind the rearmost seat does seem to lend itself to the reception of some sort of receptacle," wrote McKenna.

These points were contained in a memo sent to Durrant on 13th February 1952, a copy also being sent to A B B Valentine, showing that he was taking an interest in details of the new design from an early stage. Valentine replied to McKenna on 20th February. This memo shows that the matter of the 'To and from' board was one that he had raised. He doubted however that any mechanical device would receive the reliable co-operation of the driver. He also said he would be surprised if the operating managers did not object to the proposal for a used ticket box on the top deck, it being essential for passengers to retain their tickets until they reached the platform. He suggested instead that a second used ticket box should be built into the rear of the bus downstairs. This proved to be the only suggestion from this exercise to be adopted.

A memo dated 1st December 1951 envisaged an initial requirement for the new bus design of about 2,000 vehicles; 1,976 for trolleybus replacement, 100 estimated for augmentation of services, 146 for the replacement of the 2RT2s, 65 for the post-war STDs, 20 for the post-war Country STLs and one for G 436. The 2RT2s were scheduled for withdrawal in 1957 and the other types between 1958 and 1960, so their replacement would probably have been made by RTs released from those existing bus routes that were to be combined with former trolleybus routes and converted to RM. At this stage no allowance was being made for the greater seating capacity of the new bus, replacement of buses being anticipated on a one-for-one basis. However, in 1952 the potential savings in buses and crews began to be considered and a working party was set up to look at the economies that could be made, if all 56-seater buses, both in the Central Area and the Country Area, were replaced by 64-seaters.

The working party's report, presented to the Executive in January 1953, began with the simple arithmetic: 448 seats could be provided either by either eight 56-seater buses or seven 64-seater buses. The ability to reduce numbers of buses was however governed by other factors, principally the undesirability of making reductions where the frequency of service in the peak hours was already less than ten minutes and the need in the Country Area to maintain clockface timetables where these existed. Twenty central bus routes and fourteen groups of Country Bus routes were looked at to see what savings, in reality, could be made. These proved to be somewhat less than the theoretical savings, which nevertheless formed the conclusion to the report; i.e. an increase in seating from 56 to 64 would mean a 12.5% saving in buses, which at the beginning of 1953 would number 572. If standing passengers were taken into account, the increase in capacity would be from 61 to 69, a decrease in buses of 11.6% or 530. If the opportunity were taken with a 64-seater bus to do away with standing passengers, the increased capacity of three would give a theoretical saving of 4.7% or 214 buses.

This last matter is one that had been given consideration. Much had been done to ease the job of the bus driver over the years, but not much to ease the conductor's job. The conductor's movement through the lower saloon of the bus was much impeded by standing passengers, so from the points of view of making his job more pleasant and the efficient collection of fares, the idea of bringing an end to standing had quite a lot in its favour. This was one of the options for the new bus. In 1951 the total annual loss of revenue from fares evasion on road services was estimated at one million pounds, a large sum at that time. A start had been made on reducing transactions involving halfpennies, which often required change to be given, and the new 'Gibson' ticket machine would further assist.

Mention was made earlier of London's first eight-foot wide motor buses, the RTWs. In November 1950 a memorandum was submitted to the Executive recommending that all RT production be switched to the wider design from 1952. The trial use of RTWs on a number of central London routes between May and July 1950 had convinced both the Metropolitan and City police that their extra width was not the problem they had imagined it would be and so London Transport was happy that there would not be much difficulty in obtaining approval for the use of 8ft wide buses on most of the routes they would want to put them on. Production for 1951 was already fully committed to the 7ft 6ins version, but it would be possible to change over to the 8ft width from the following year. The memorandum, signed by Durrant and the two Operating Managers (Central and Country), recommended that production be switched to the 8ft version as soon as possible, with 1,781 being supplied on AEC chassis between 1952 and 1954 and 425 on Leyland chassis. AEC undertook to redesign the RT3 chassis so that it could be interchangeable with the Leyland 8ft chassis insofar as body mounting was concerned. Leyland offered to release the drawings and special tools for the production of their design of body so that it could be manufactured by other body builders. Had this plan proceeded, over 2,500 eight-foot wide buses would have been in London service by the time RM 1 was launched.

In Durrant's own Words

A A M (Albert Arthur Molteno) Durrant was head of the design team at London Transport's Chiswick Works that developed the Routemaster. His own account of the work done was recorded for posterity soon after RM 1 entered service.

We decided to start from rock bottom and make a complete reassessment, not only of the engineering aspect of the design but of the operating specification – the operating requirement for the new vehicle. It is very necessary to have a complete reappraisal from time to time, otherwise one can run in a groove and repeat features of design or items in the original requirement which really are out-of-date. No doubt they were there for a good purpose when first thought of, but they tend to become almost traditional features of the design and it does not always occur to anyone to question or alter them.

The first thing to do then, in considering the new Routemaster design, was to make a complete reappraisal of the operating requirements, and we asked the Operating Managers to try and erase from their minds all past features they had specified, to think out their requirements from rock-bottom and ignore for the time being any restrictions that hitherto may have had an influence upon them, such as Ministry regulations, the aim being to get down to the ideal bus from their point of view. If necessary, we would go into the question of seeking some relaxation or other in the regulations later on.

The first thing questioned was whether the new vehicle should be a double decker or a single decker – a very fundamental question. The answer to that was clear; it should be a double decker. The reason is that if we try to carry as many people in a single decker as in a double decker, there must be a high proportion of standees. Quite apart from any question as to whether the platform staff are going to be prepared to accept a high proportion of standees, our view, and the operating view, is that a high-proportion standee vehicle is going to lower the standard of passenger appeal.

Another reason for deciding upon the double decker was that the road area occupied by a double decker is less than by a single decker for the same capacity; the vehicle is much shorter, much more manoeuvrable, and can cater better for the congested traffic which we have to face, particularly when getting away from the pavement around a line of parked cars.

The next point to decide was whether we should have a front entrance, a middle entrance or a rear entrance. Should there be two entrances? Should the staircase be at the rear, in the middle or at the front? All these possibilities were carefully studied.

The question of the time of loading and unloading has a very important bearing upon efficiency. If a door is provided, it is inevitable that the time of loading and unloading is going to be increased. This was one of the things we wanted to avoid at all costs, and so, having decided that we could not tolerate doors on our double-deck buses in London, a front or middle entrance was precluded because, with either, it would not be safe to operate without a door. Having decided that we must have a rear entrance, it followed that we must also have a rear staircase, because a rear loading platform with a staircase anywhere else would inevitably incur a congestion of people trying to go inside and upstairs at the same time.

Facing page On 9th August 1949, Durrant presented to the Executive a memorandum on a new double decker that had been designed by AEC and in which AEC were keen to interest London Transport. It was expected to become the successor to the AEC Regent III. The arrangement of the engine, transmission and chassis was similar to that on AEC's recently developed underfloor engined single decker, a design used for the 700-strong fleet of RFs built between 1951 and 1953. AEC claimed the following advantages: 60 seats within an overall length of 27ft, improved suspension, full-fronted body construction and 'silent operation'. The following January Durrant reported that: "Our own research into the general question of double-deck bus design for the future has included a close study of the possibilities of the under-floor engine . . . Whilst it is strongly advocated that opportunity be taken of making a practical study of the under-floor double-deck arrangement, it might be premature were inference drawn therefrom that this basic type of vehicle is necessarily the precursor of our next step forward in standard design. Present indications tend to the contrary."

The next question was whether we should have the engine at the front, under the floor, or at the rear. Since we had decided upon a rear entrance, clearly if we put the engine at the rear we should be reducing our platform space or, alternatively, shortening the length and therefore the passenger capacity of the lower saloon. If we put the engine under the floor, inevitably the vehicle must be higher because of the need to accommodate a minimum diameter of engine flywheel, and even with a local protuberance through the floor under a seat, in practice the result would have been a higher floor, a higher ceiling and therefore a higher vehicle. We cannot tolerate a higher vehicle however because of the many height-restricting bridges.

Considering the front of the vehicle, could we use the space on the nearside of the driver for any useful purpose? The answer is no, because if passengers are accommodated in that corner we immediately have difficulty with driver's visibility. The earliest of the fully-fronted trolleybuses had passenger seats right up at the front. This arrangement was found unworkable. We also tried, just before the war, a fully fronted STL bus, to see whether we could improve the appearance value. We found, however, that it was deficient from the point of view of driver's visibility compared with the half front and, indeed, we were obliged to remove it from the experimental vehicle.

Granted these things, there is nothing for which you can use the front nearside corner, and therefore it might just as well be used to accommodate the engine. That is the reason why, in the Routemaster vehicle, the engine remains in what is, to us, the orthodox position. In some respects, the Routemaster looks disappointingly like an RT bus; it is not because we have studiously copied or followed the tradition of the RT type of bus, but because of certain fundamental reasons which we re-explored and confirmed as being sound.

The appearance of the rear-entrance Crossley body was an odd and ungainly-looking mixture of London Transport and Birmingham Corporation practice, with hints of the RT in the curved profile, half-drop windows and destination blind equipment, whilst the thick upper-deck corner pillars and continuous rain-strip over the side windows were Birmingham characteristics – the Crossley body shop was engaged in a large contract for that undertaking at the time. The weight proved excessive and a lighter and neater 64-seat replacement body was built by Park Royal, evidently intended for the 1950 Show, but the whole project was dropped and the vehicle dismantled. What the project had shown however, was that 64 seats could be fitted into a length of 27ft.

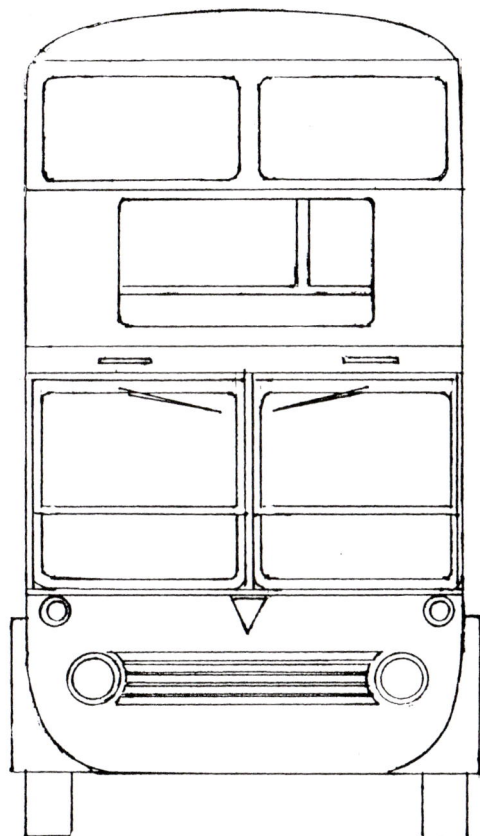

The next important point in the operating requirement was: how many people should be carried on the new vehicle? That, of course, is a vital question, and consequently a considerable amount of operational research was undertaken on the subject. The outcome satisfied the Operators that in no circumstances did they want more than 70 passengers, including standees, which, in effect, meant that they did not want seating for more than 65 passengers. The reason for that is two-fold. First, in London, as the statistics show, there is a large proportion of short-riding passengers. With that state of affairs, the larger the vehicle the greater are the delays at the stopping places to enable passengers to get on and off. In consequence, if you carry more than a certain number of people, you slow the vehicle down and, to provide a given service, you require more buses although they are bigger. Second, the larger the capacity, the more difficult becomes the collection of fares.

Summarising, we arrived at these basic facts: It was to be a double-decker with rear entrance and stairs and with engine at the front; it was to carry not more than 65 seated passengers. There was also the question of length, and here the Operators pressed that the existing length should not be exceeded more than was absolutely necessary. Even in the early stages, before there was any question of a concession of 30ft length for the double decker, all were agreed that we should not, in any case, take advantage of 30ft, but should retain as short a length as possible to facilitate manoeuvrability, to reduce congestion caused by our own vehicles, and particularly to ease the driver's task in the general congestion and in getting round the parked cars and vans.

At the juncture then reached the length regulation was 27ft for a double decker, and we decided that before approaching the Ministry to seek any further concessions, we would see what we could do within the existing regulation length, particularly as we were desirous of keeping the vehicles as short as we could. We found that if we squared up the front of the upper saloon we could set the front seats in the upper deck forward slightly and then, by giving the same spacing of seats on the upper deck as we have in the lower deck, we could, taking the upper and the lower saloons together, accommodate a total of 64 passengers within 27ft 6ins. We, therefore, looked around to see what we could do, and found that there is 6 inches occupied by the radiator and the fan at the front, so that if we could locate these underneath the vehicles as we have them on the RF vehicles, we could accommodate 64 passengers, only one short of the 65 specified, within the then prevailing legal length.

The next question which arose was this: if we were going to increase the passenger accommodation in the way I have described, it would mean adding six more passengers on the upper deck and two more in the lower deck. It was highly desirable in any case to reduce as much as possible the total weight of the vehicle to ensure conformity with the regulation weight and also to minimise fuel consumption, tyre wear, and so on, but we had also to contend with the regulation tilting angle. With the road surface tilted to 28° with a full load on top only, a double decker must still remain stable. We only just got by with the RTs, so something had to be done to ensure the tilt with a larger proportion of top passenger load.

We concluded that the lightest construction would be of the chassisless type, in which the structure would be made completely self-supporting, a self contained box, with a deep girder construction formed in the sides of the vehicle, having the mechanical units planted underneath. To do this, and to do it the lightest possible way, we realised we had to do something about the suspension, particularly at the front, because with the normal solid front axle the front bulkhead is subjected to a tremendous amount of wracking. So we decided to go for independent suspension at the front. Another aim was at all costs to get away from leaf springs because leaf springs are very unreliable things; they are extremely costly – over the life of the vehicle the money spent upon them is something like a quarter of that spent on engine maintenance.

We also had to do something with the suspension to help us on the question of stability. After examining many alternative possibilities, we decided upon the suspension frame arrangement. It consists of two side or torque members, pivoted at the forward end about half-way along the length of the vehicle, to which the rear axle is attached through rubber sandwiches. Continuing rearwards, a cross-member is attached to their ends and passes right across to the sides of the vehicle; at which point it carries two coil springs. The idea was to carry the points of suspension right to the sides of the vehicle. The farther outwards you can take the suspension the more stable the vehicle becomes.

Thus, we decided on independent suspension at the front and the special form of suspension at the back, both provided with shock absorbers which are essential with any form of coil spring. Tests have shown that with full top load only we can get a tilting angle of 32°, as compared with the regulation figure of 28°.

The next question was what material should be used for the main structure of the new vehicle. There was steel, which undoubtedly can offer very light weight construction, or there was light alloy – aluminium alloy – to choose from. We chose light alloy, mainly because to obtain light weight structure in steel, it is necessary to use very thin section metal for the pillars. With light alloy, however, which is of lower density, for the same weight you can have an appreciably thicker section.

With thin section steel, an attack of rust, possibly somewhere unseen, has only the thin section to corrode before the part will fail. Light alloy, with its thicker section, even if corrosion does set in, stands much less chance of failure. Further to this, we have already satisfied ourselves that, with proper treatment, aluminium alloy can be thoroughly protected from corrosion, so that, of the two materials, light alloy could be regarded as the most reliable. Light alloy was, therefore, decided upon, and the whole of the structure is in that material. Indeed, the only ferrous material used is for the mechanical units, axles and certain of the main members. We wanted to avoid the use of wood and so the flooring, everything in the body structure, is of light alloy material.

At the Works at Aldenham and, before that, at Chiswick, our procedure for overhauling vehicles has always been to remove the body from the chassis so that the two components can be dealt with separately. Interchangeability between bodies and chassis throughout means that the same body need not go back on the same chassis, and this feature is of importance in securing maximum economy in the overhauling process.

In the case of the Routemaster, having resolved to adopt a chassisless design, the question arose as to how could we make that fit in with the provisions at our overhaul works for removing the body? To depart from the system that we are working today and try to overhaul the vehicle in one entity would not only upset our provisions, facilities and equipment, but would inevitably take longer because there is a limit to the number of men you can get round a vehicle, and it would not be possible to deal with the vehicle as a whole as quickly as by making some kind of diversion between the mechanical parts and the structure itself.

So we had to work out a means for meeting that particular problem, and we solved it by providing for the front portion of the vehicle, including the axle, engine and steering, to be assembled on two special members which could, with ease, be attached to and removed from the body structure by releasing a limited number of king bolts.

In the case of the rear suspension, the springs are first withdrawn – with coil springs this is a simple matter – then the shackle pins are withdrawn from the forward end of the suspension members, which enables the rear assembly to be run out as a complete unit. Having removed the forward and rear assemblies, we are left with the body structure and the only remaining mechanical unit, the gearbox, which is not normally removed at Aldenham in any case. So, in effect, we resolved the problem of the integral body by making it capable of rapid disintegration, which constitutes an important feature of the Routemaster design.

The Routemaster design also embodies a number of other lightweight features; for example, the passenger seats comprise stainless steel frames with fibreglass seat backs. I will not go into further detail, but a lot of thought has been put into means designed to keep the weight to the lowest possible limit. Actual experiments with the prototypes have shown that the expected improvement in fuel consumption deriving from the reduction in weight is achieved; in other words, the fuel consumption in miles per gallon of the Routemaster vehicle carrying 64 passengers is slightly better than that of the RT carrying only 56 passengers.

The next thing was a consideration of the general performance of the vehicle and what we could do still further to ease the task of the driver and of the conductor. As concerns the driver, the greatest physical exertion which he is called upon to make is to steer the vehicle. Over the years we have improved things in a number of ways. Taking the RT, compared with the previous types, the gear selector and pedal change operation require no effort at all; the brakes which the driver used to apply by direct force and then with servo assistance, today are applied by an air pedal with no exertion. But we have not so far effected an improvement proportionately with the steering and so, in the new vehicle, we are providing power assistance for the steering. This has become more necessary in these days, largely once again because of parked cars; the bus stops being at the side of the road, the driver must immediately turn out under slow motion to get clear of them. The power assistance is applied in such a way that, whilst it does not make the steering wheel finger-light, it considerably eases the steering, the object being two-fold; first, if we provide very easy steering we may tempt some of our racing drivers to tear around corners and incur a risk. Second, in the event of failure of the power servo mechanism, we do not want to be left with too big a difference in feel, i.e. from a very easy turn to a relatively stiff turn, again in the interests of safety.

So far as transmission is concerned, there is a general trend towards fully automatic transmission. From our point of view we feel that, whilst relieving the driver still further, automatic transmission is going to give better performance, better service from the vehicle running point of view and in respect of passenger comfort, than manual control.

But there is one important feature in the gearbox of this automatic transmission, namely, the feature of sustained torque. This means that there is a perfectly smooth transition from one gear to another even when changing up with the foot right down on the accelerator pedal. With the ordinary pre-selective transmission we have today, when changing up you have to lift your foot off the accelerator pedal, change and then apply it again. Unfortunately, some of our drivers do not do this, with the result that many of our passengers are severely jerked. With the now sustained torque feature, the accelerator can be kept down all the time when changing up without a jerk at all. This is done by independent operation of the bands on the epicyclic trains, so that one band is held on until the other is applied. The constant transmission of power in this fashion alone gives an improvement in acceleration of some 8%, which is obtained for nothing, the reason being that by keeping the accelerator pedal down you avoid any drop in momentum of the engine which has to be picked up again, the same thing applying to the momentum of the vehicle itself, which is not checked and therefore does not have to be accelerated again.

I now come to the brakes. We have given a lot of thought to brakes because, in compressed air braking as used on the RT, such troubles as we experience with them are usually due to the grit under valves – dirt, rust, and that sort of thing, and with freezing in very cold weather. So we decided to equip the new vehicles with hydraulic braking – pressure hydraulic throughout – with safety provision for isolation of the front and rear brakes. This system, in addition to eliminating the hazard of grit getting under valves and eliminating freezing trouble, gives a very pleasant characteristic of brake application; finally it offers a complete system of very much lighter weight.

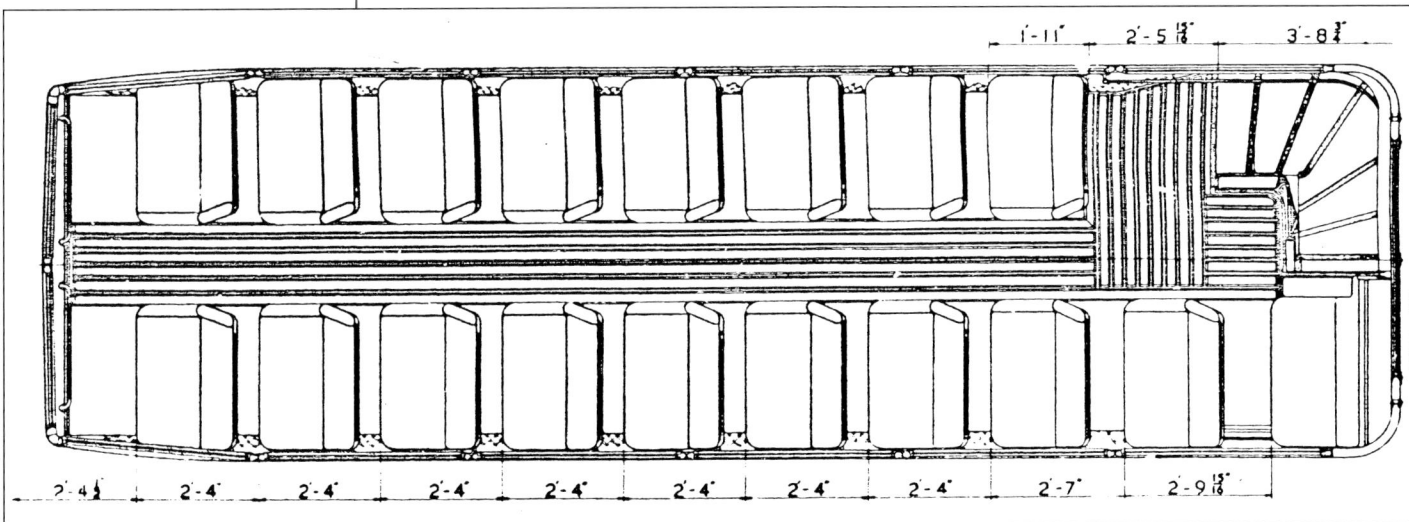

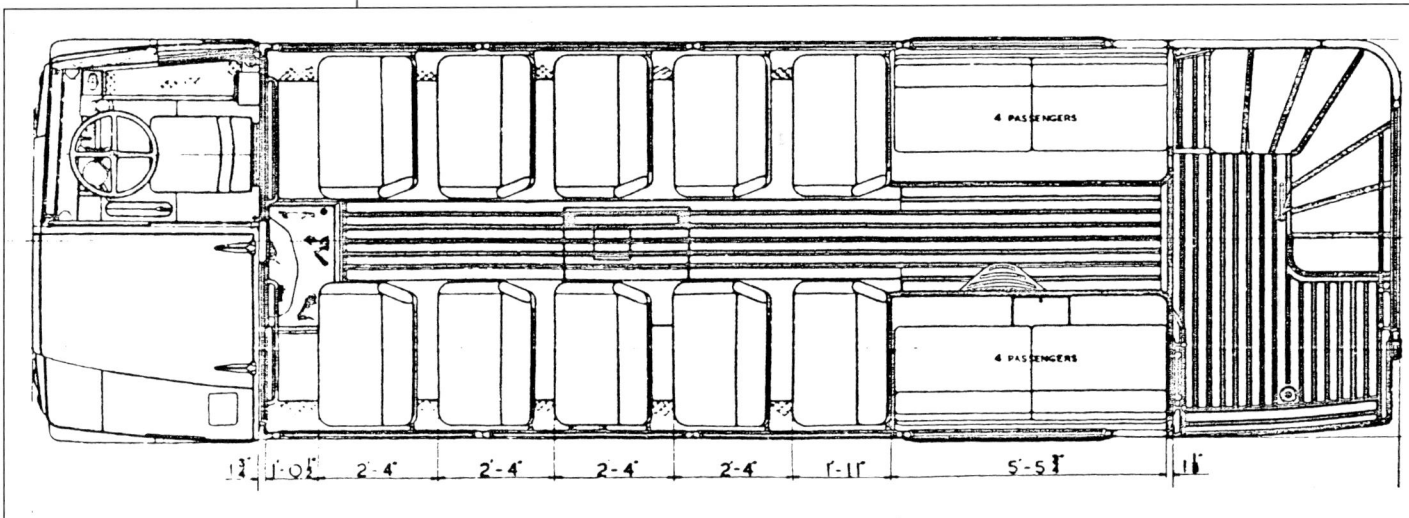

Upper and lower deck seating layouts for the RM. Compared with the RT, six more passengers were accommodated upstairs and two more downstairs.

Summarising, the Routemaster offers enhanced passenger appeal in terms of a much more comfortable ride resulting from the improved form of suspension; the elimination of transmission jerks, particularly with the automatic gear change; greater freedom of movement by reason of increased gangway width and better visibility by using 'quarter-drop' windows instead of 'half-drop' which tend to cut across the line of vision.

For the driver, the cab design which offers excellent visibility, is much improved both as regards space and as regards the design and placing of the controls, both of these features being the outcome of comprehensive physical/medical study. Mental and physical strain upon the driver can be further reduced by the simplified gear change and power assisted steering.

For the conductor, the wider gangways materially ease the task of fare collection; the provision of a recess beneath the stairs enables the conductor to stand clear of passengers entering and leaving the saloon, thus adding to his comfort and the freedom of passenger movement.

13

Designing the Body

Once the essential elements had been decided, attention could turn to the visual aspects of the body design. For this a consultant, Douglas Scott, was called in to assist. The classic design that was the finished product was the result of Durrant's team and Scott working together.

The basic shape of the new bus was the responsibility of Durrant's team at Chiswick. This was finalised by early 1952. The bus would be just over one foot longer than the RT, taking advantage of the maximum legal permitted length of 27ft and the maximum permitted width of 8ft. It would accommodate 64 passengers by careful spacing of the interior. The RM seated six more passengers on the upper deck and two more downstairs when compared with the RT. The greater length of the RM and a quarter inch reduction in seat spacing on the lower deck enabled bench seats over the rear axle to each seat four passengers instead of three. On the upper deck, the upright front end, a reduced space at the top of the stairs and 1¼ inches less space between seats permitted an extra pair of seats on the nearside and an extra two pairs on the offside. This combination gave 14% more seating in a bus 5% longer.

During the first half of 1952 an industrial design partnership, Scott Ashford Associates, was called in to advise on the visual aspects of the design. Douglas Scott and Fred Ashford had formed this consultancy in 1949 and Scott had recently done some work on the RF for London Transport. It was Douglas Scott who made the necessary frequent visits to Chiswick in 1952 to help with the mock-up; Fred Ashford took little interest in bus design.

Douglas Scott's main input into the external design of the Routemaster was in the handling of curves on what was basically a flat sided box and designing a bonnet within the constraints of the mechanical parts that would need to be housed under it. The length of the bonnet and the size and the position of the entrance were among the items decided by Durrant's team, as was the fact that the sides would not curve in at the bottom so that the bus would be better suited to the new bus washing machines being introduced at garages.

Scott suggested a full front for the new bus when he was first called in and showed some sketches (long since lost) to London Transport. Designers were keen on the idea of full fronts for buses because of the neater appearance; as we have seen, AEC's own hoped for successor to the RT had incorporated one also. Practical considerations – particularly the driver's view of the nearside – ruled this out so far as London Transport was concerned and the traditional half-cab was specified.

Following the lead of RTC 1, Scott designed a full-width bonnet extending over the front nearside wheel that, with modifications, was used on RMs 1 and 2. The bonnet needed much subsequent work as the mechanical specification of the RM changed, and Douglas Scott was brought back in 1955 to help with the bonnet and grille for the second two prototypes and again in 1956 when something different was required for the production vehicles. Scott was never fully happy with the final version. In a letter to the writer in 1990, he wrote that "the top line of the bonnet had to be modified to accommodate a power-steering header tank, giving it that broken-backed appearance which has become so familiar that no-one notices it except me".

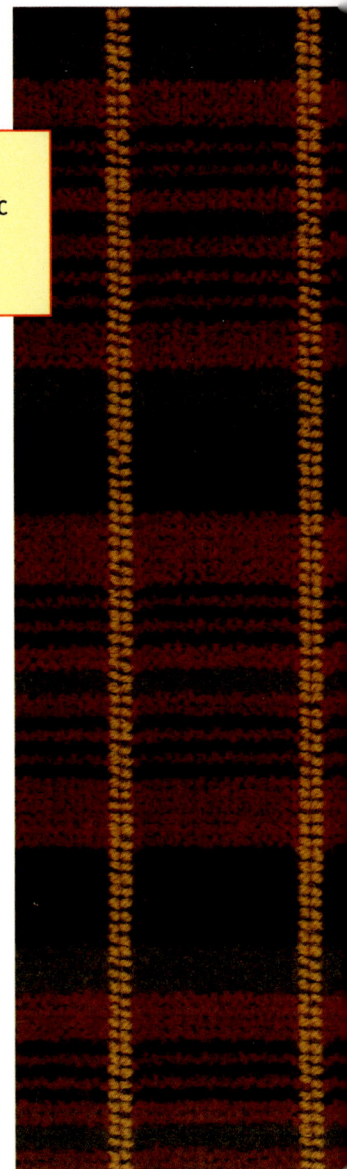

Above Douglas Scott's design for the seat moquette.

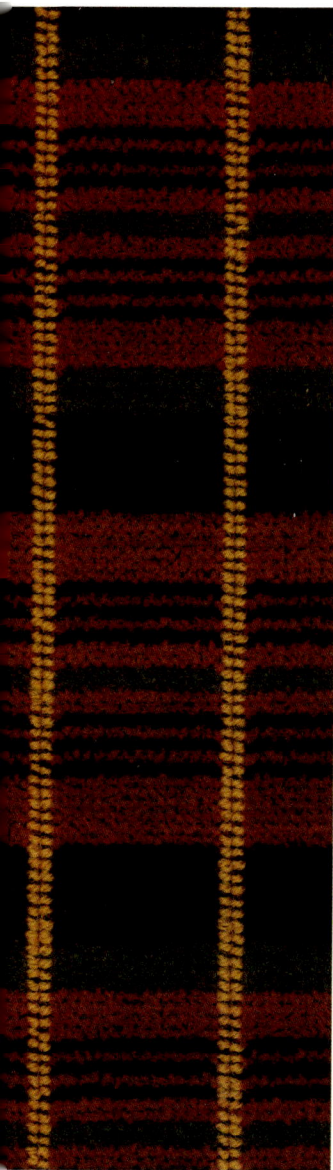

Above right The first complete model of the new body was made in June 1952. The upright front was quite a departure from previous and contemporary practice.

Scott had a bit more freedom inside the bus, but an idea of his for solid fibreglass seat frames and handrails was rejected because it was found that they would be heavier than light alloy tubing (platform handrails were traditional stainless steel). He also envisaged fluorescent lighting panels set into the ceiling, an idea rejected on the grounds of initial cost and more time-consuming maintenance. The interior colour scheme was largely Scott's, but a suggestion that the Sung yellow ceiling colour be extended to the top third of the window frames was not adopted. His design for the seating moquette proved very successful. The dominant deep red was very hardwearing and the yellow vertical stripes, Scott explained, were designed to give the seats a bright appearance even after a few years of use. The same design of moquette was still being fitted as standard to Routemasters until 1992. Scott was also credited with the 'sentry box' under the stairs where the conductor could stand out of the way of passengers boarding and alighting.

Above left The first full size mock-up of the front end of the new bus was completed in the Chiswick experimental shop in spring 1952. The precise date this photograph was taken is not known as, rather unhelpfully, Chiswick photos tended to have the date of printing stamped on the back rather than the date of taking. The first modification of this design was a minor change to the bonnet, giving it a more bulbous top (photo on page 2). It shows the dummy grille that LT management thought looked too much like that of a trolleybus.

Above right In this version, the grille has been raised and redesigned, but more significantly the area around it projects beyond the rest of the bus – a change that was to remain a feature of RM 1's design and may have been part of the answer to the criticism of trolleybus styling, though the main reason for the change is more likely to have been a need for more space for the mechanical parts. On 5th June 1952 Durrant had viewed the previous version with its RT style destination display and requested a review of the destination equipment with the intention of saving weight. The blind display shown here was the result.

Above left Later in 1952 the grille had been completely redesigned with vertical slats replacing the horizontal ones and the registration number moved to below it. Though looking more like a bus radiator than the previous designs, the grille would still have been a dummy one as throughout RM 1's development the radiator was to have been an underfloor fitment in order to save space.

Above right Not totally satisfied with Douglas Scott's attempts, Durrant's team – possibly working on a suggestion by Executive member A B B Valentine – came up with the front 'grille' design that was to be used at first on RM 1. It was inspected by Durrant on 8th May 1953 and was modified on the bus itself, with chrome verticals replacing the red and an extra one being added in the middle. The London Transport bullseye became red outlined in cream, rather than black outlined in red, to produce a pleasing appearance.

AEC and the Routemaster

Alan Townsin worked in the drawing office of AEC's Southall factory when, in one part of it, the mechanical components were being worked on. AEC was London Transport's natural partner in bus design and here Alan writes about the contribution the company made to the development of the Routemaster.

I cannot claim to have had any part in the design of the Routemaster, even though I was in AEC's drawing office at its Southall works in 1951–55 and hence there during the period when the firm's design work on the mechanical aspects of the prototype was done. The office was divided into 'the design side' and 'the production side' and I was one of the latter team. We rarely had any excuse for straying into the area occupied by the senior design staff and, indeed, were not encouraged to do so – knowledge of what might be the firm's future products was what would nowadays be called commercially sensitive information. The whole building, with the experimental department occupying the ground floor below us, was out of bounds for other employees or visitors, except with specific permission. Even so, with a lively interest in what was going on, one took the odd peek at what was on the various drawing boards as opportunity offered.

Probably at some date around 1952–53, I can clearly remember spotting a drawing of the front end of what was clearly a front-engined bus chassis having independent front suspension. By that date, this feature was usual for cars but still virtually unknown on any kind of bus, where the traditional beam axle was still universal on production models not just at AEC but across the whole industry – indeed, 60 years or so later, the latter is still very common.

So that was intriguing, but what I had not at first grasped was that what I, at first glance, took to be a drawing of just the front-end of the chassis was in fact the complete front sub-frame assembly, with the engine, driver's controls and front suspension, for incorporation into a vehicle of integral construction. I remember noticing the selector lever assembly on the steering column, looking quite like the RT version for that model's preselective gearbox though not quite the same and in fact controlling an example of the new-generation epicyclic gearbox which eliminated the 'clutch' (actually gear-change) pedal. No radiator was shown in front of the engine but that did not seem significant as work on the drawing was still in hand.

We all knew that a new double decker was in course of design for the London Transport Executive, as the organisation was at that date. Regular liaison with that organisation was simply part of normal life – for example, the LTE's engineering department at Chiswick automatically received copies of all alteration notes detailing changes to any item used on AEC passenger models, regardless of whether the type in question was used in the LTE fleet. There were historic reasons for the close links, and about half of AEC's output had been in fulfilling the slogan 'Builders of London's buses'. The staff more directly involved made regular visits to Chiswick and it became known that the prototype of the new bus for LTE was being assembled there and that there was parallel involvement by Park Royal in regard to the bodywork.

To understand AEC's role in the development of the Routemaster, it is important to recall how the firm began and the nature of its relationship to London bus operation. What was then called the Associated Equipment Co Ltd was formed in June 1912 to take over bus chassis production at the works at Walthamstow, on the eastern outskirts of London, already in full flow under the direct ownership of the London General Omnibus Co Ltd. The latter was by far the largest bus operator in the London area, and the works was supplying its needs for motor bus chassis. Both LGOC and AEC were to remain Underground subsidiaries until the newly-formed London Passenger Transport Board, a public authority set up by Act of Parliament, took over responsibility for the operation of public transport in the London area from 1st July 1933.

The agreement between LPTB and AEC on chassis supply was revised in form but still gave a commitment to large-scale chassis supply from AEC after the end of the 1939–45 war. In regard to bodywork, it was decided to adopt a new policy of designing the entire structure based on full-sized drawings produced at Chiswick, using a system evolved from aircraft work. This enabled the RT3 bodies, identical to the last detail, to be produced by Park Royal and Weymann using the same sets of drawings.

When the time came for the RT, in turn, to be succeeded by a new design, the LPTB's successor, the London Transport Executive, had new factors and possibilities to bear in mind, many of them based on experimental work already involving AEC. Technology had advanced since the mid-1930s when the initial planning for the RT had been carried out. Further development of the Wilson-type preselective gearbox into a semi- and then fully automatic transmission system had been in hand from about that same period, some early work involving STL-type buses. Work on adapting the type of hydraulic system used on aircraft to operate a bus braking system began soon after the 1939–45 war.

The adoption of what was then usually called chassisless construction on trolleybuses, jointly developed with AEC and the bodybuilders concerned in 1939–40, was an obvious basis for further progress on similar lines. Following the decision to standardise on motor buses long-term, an interest in increasing seating capacity from the hitherto standard figure of 56 a little nearer to the 70 usual for London trolleybuses, was another aim. Slightly increased maximum permissible dimensions for two-axle double deckers of 27ft long and 8ft wide (the latter already permitted but only on a route approval basis) came into effect from 1950 and were helpful in this respect and a seating capacity of 64 was chosen. Reduction of weight, important as a key to lower operating costs, together with improved ride comfort to make bus travel more attractive, were other considerations.

These aims were set out in a document dated 9th November 1951 and a small team began work in a corner of the Technical Office at Chiswick, soon working with similarly small teams from AEC and the Park Royal Vehicles bodybuilding concern, the latter involved as the largest supplier of bodies to London Transport post-war – by then, it was also financially associated with AEC. At that stage, the RT was still in full-scale production, with about eight chassis coming off AEC's production line every week, augmented by Leyland manufacture of RTL chassis. The all-important early stages of detailed development work were again carried out jointly with London's traditional bus supplier, AEC.

The relevant positions and functions of the LTE, AEC and PRV members of this small group of engineers need brief explanation. As the user, LTE clearly knew what it wanted, yet even its wishes had to be tempered by the legal requirements covering vehicle design as well as the manufacturing and operating practicalities, not least in terms of cost. Undoubtedly, its own engineers, led by the visionary and vastly experienced A A M Durrant, who had been London Transport's senior engineer in charge of bus design under slightly varying titles since 1933, could have directly directed the necessary design work. Assembling a large enough team of suitably qualified designers and draughtsmen would have required a large-scale recruitment exercise, but that would be only one of the hurdles to surmount.

The advantage of involving AEC and PRV was not only that of involving people with specialised expertise in such matters as engines, gearboxes or body structures already in the senior posts within those firms' own design teams. It also brought knowledge of the availability of existing standard parts suitable for incorporation or bought-in items and their capabilities. There was also valuable access to production knowledge and experience of manufacturing methods and costs. Beyond AEC's or PRV's own organisation, this gave liaison with suppliers of such items as castings, forgings and the extrusions found in modern body structures. In other words, it gave access to a vast hinterland of specialised knowledge, including that of concerns such as the makers of brake or electrical equipment who would best be able to advise on specific problems in those specialised fields.

However, designing a bus as a complete entity to suit the needs of one operator had major advantages as compared to normal commercial design of a vehicle for general sale, where the aim is to suit a variety of customers' requirements with inevitable uncertainties as to body variations and the type of use, operating conditions, etc.

Odd though it may seem at first thought, in some senses the initial planning work can proceed from the top down. With a precise idea of the dimensions of the upper deck and the numbers of passengers and seats, the weight and stresses to be borne by the lower part of the vehicle structure become more precisely defined and this, in turn, with the lower deck occupants and contents, leads to clearer choices on mechanical components and the weight to be carried by the suspension at each end of the vehicle, right down to the appropriate tyre size and specification. The cumulative effect of weight savings, each tending to allow other associated items to be lighter, helped to allow the overall saving to be greater.

Once the size and weight of the bus was known sufficiently clearly, it became evident that an engine of similar power and general characteristics to that used in the RT would fit the requirement. Bearing in mind that AEC's 9.6-litre engine had first been introduced to suit London Transport's specification, and of which there would soon be 4,674 of the A204 version in service in post-war RT-type buses, it was an obvious choice for the first Routemaster, where the engine fitted was almost unaltered, apart from installation differences. In the event, this proved not to be the unit used for production Routemasters when regular output began in 1958, AEC by then having moved on to the AV590 engine, differing in many respects even though of the same 9.6-litre size.

At AEC, a general switch, applying to all its fluid-transmission passenger models, was about to be made from the preselective type of Wilson epicyclic gearbox to what was sometimes called the direct-selection type, which responded immediately to movement of the control lever, rather than to a pedal movement made when the change was required, which was the characteristic feature of a preselector. The drawings for this came in from Self-Changing Gears Ltd, which was the company founded by Wilson to be responsible for development but not capable of large-scale production, which would be handled at AEC's works at Southall. Basically similar work linked to SCG was in hand at Leyland, which had decided that epicyclic gearboxes were needed for some important passenger vehicle markets.

With the RT, London Transport, and hence AEC, had made use of an air-pressure brake system for a motor bus a practical everyday proposition, and eventually the rest of the industry generally followed suit, although often many years later. Hydraulic operation of brakes, though coupled to a vacuum servo, had been standard on the STL and other vehicles in the 1930s, but air pressure had given more braking power although with an inherent delay effect. Using a hydraulic pump system developed by Lockheed for the Routemaster gave very responsive operation. I think it is fair to say that London Transport engineers felt they had again stepped forward a generation, though on this occasion the rest of the industry was less keen, perhaps because some of the parts were very expensive at first, and AEC did not offer power-hydraulic braking on other models.

Quite early in 1954, preliminary plans for the firm's exhibits at the Commercial Motor Show became known, and that the new London bus – the name 'Routemaster' was not revealed until just before the Show – was to be among them. I continued to be involved in other matters, notably the updated more conventional Regent V series of double-deck chassis derived from the Regent III, also being introduced in time for that Show. However, at a date I regret not recording but probably at some time in late August, the prototype, later known as RM 1, with paintwork gleaming in the sun, appeared at Southall and pulled up outside the main entrance to the drawing office, this being the first time it had been seen at AEC's works. The temptation to go and look at it was strong, but then the word went round that we – all drawing office staff present – were to go downstairs and board it to be taken for a ride.

This was an unprecedented event, and the only such occasion in the four years I worked there. So far as I recall, the ride only went as far as the main entrance gate, with a circuit of the square of grass with flagpole visible in many official pictures of AEC vehicles, en route, although the brief run did involve going down the tree-lined drive extending for perhaps a quarter of a mile parallel to what was then the British Railways Western Region main line. A turning loop was provided just short of the gateway and we turned back there, very probably because the vehicle was on trade plates, ruling out running on the road with passengers. Even so, we were probably the first full passenger load, other than perhaps London Transport employees, to ride in a Routemaster – the bus did not enter public service until February 1956 and production examples not until June 1959.

Just quite why we were invited to take that very brief trip is not clear – it was not the firm's habit to indulge its staff in such ways but it was certainly appreciated by several employees, not least the author of this reminiscence, and comes back as a clear memory 48 years later. Initial impressions were mostly favourable, though I do recall misgivings in view of the reduced weight – the trend towards lighter vehicles had been evident since the 1952 Show, with the MCW Orion body as perhaps the best-known example, let down by its crude and austere interior and generally 'tinny' character. That was certainly not evident on RM 1, beyond very slight 'give' in the flooring noted on that occasion. The standard of interior finish, continued in the production examples, set a standard I still feel has not been surpassed among city buses.

Even so, I recall predicting that the type probably wouldn't last as well as the RT, reasoning that cutting about three-quarters of a ton on this 64-seat 27ft by 8ft bus as compared to the 56-seat 26ft by 7ft 6in RT must surely have implied some compromise with durability. Viewed from 50 years later, I have to eat those words and salute the skill of the body structure design engineers in particular.

That brief trip was too short to be able to make more than general judgement. The engine on that vehicle was the existing AEC 9.6 litre unit, very similar to the A204 type as used on the RT, so sounding and behaving much the same. Although the gearbox was new, its internal epicyclic gearing was also generally similar to that of an RT, so the overall sound effects under normal acceleration seemed much the same. The RT still set better standards in this respect than many other bus models then in production, so their continuation in a vehicle of lighter construction was reassuring. There wasn't an opportunity to draw any conclusions on such matters as the effect of the new suspension at the modest speeds over what were quite smooth roadways within the works area.

A technical description of the new model was issued as a press notice by London Transport dated 25th August 1954, but embargoed so as to forbid publication before the opening day of the Commercial Vehicle Show on 24th September. It is noteworthy that the description still did not refer to the vehicle by name – it was simply "London Transport's new double-deck bus". Members of the trade press were invited to view the vehicle on 25th August at Chiswick, though it does not seem that any demonstration run outside the limits of the works took place.

The first person to drive RM 1 was Bert Smith, the foreman of the Chiswick experimental shop. Late one summer evening in 1954, almost under cover of darkness, the bus trundled around the works. Staff member John Lewis witnessed the event: "The first thing I noticed was the noise from the exhaust – rather like that of an RLH. It had at that time a noisier, more guttural sound coming from the exhaust than an RT". Members of the trade press gathered at Chiswick Works on 25th August 1954 to inspect the bus. E J Smith went along as part of his duties as a member of AEC's publicity department, taking some photographs including these three views. By then he was also editing the predecessor to today's *Buses* magazine. A short trip within the grounds of Chiswick was made, those on the lower deck having to stand because no seats had yet been fitted downstairs. The small blind box above the platform was intended to display the ultimate destination only.

Other Interests

Aware that AEC and London Transport were working on something, other manufacturers did not want to be forgotten. This was particularly the case with Leyland but, less obviously, Bristol and ECW also expressed interest in being involved. Stewart J Brown writes about the approaches from companies who did not want to be left out in the cold.

In the automotive world it is not uncommon for designers and engineers to be thinking about the next new model as soon as – or even before – the current one has been launched.

And there's a parallel with London Transport and the Routemaster, which was already under development long before the last of the legendary RT class of AEC Regents had been delivered. Authority to develop a new design of double-deck bus had been given by the chairman of the London Passenger Transport Board in October 1947, when RT deliveries were in full swing.

With its new model LT was eager to maintain the standardisation which it was achieving with the RT family, as well as exploring new methods of construction to minimise unladen weight and maximise payload. It was also exploring alternative sources of supply. With the bulk of the 2,760 Routemasters which were built for London having had AEC running units in Park Royal bodies, it is easy to overlook that Leyland was a significant supplier, and that other body builders – ECW and Weymann – were involved in building the prototypes and also tendered to build production vehicles.

As design work progressed they were not the only manufacturers who were being considered by LT. Saunders Roe, which had experience in building aluminium bodies, was one whose expertise was thought worth considering, as was chassis manufacturer Bristol, which got as far as putting proposals to LT for the production of running units. Bristol was part of the state-owned British Transport Commission, set up by the postwar Labour government to manage the nationalised transport industries which included the London Transport Executive.

AEC had, historically, been the major supplier of London's bus chassis, operating from a large site at Windmill Lane in Southall where it built buses not just for London, but for operators around the world. AEC was also a major lorry manufacturer and a major exporter of trucks and buses.

Park Royal, based in the London suburb of that name, would be the biggest single builder of bodies on the RT, producing 3,280, with the last being delivered in November 1954. Its output of RT bodies averaged nearly nine a week.

As the closest major bodybuilder to AEC, Park Royal had built up a strong relationship with the chassis manufacturer. In 1949 Park Royal was purchased by Associated Commercial Vehicles, thus becoming a sister company of AEC within the ACV group.

By March 1953 progress in developing its new bus had reached the stage where LT had drawn up an agreement with AEC and Park Royal in which LT agreed to finance the development costs involved in producing two prototypes of what was simply described as "an integrated all-metal double-deck bus". From the start LT retained the right to enter into arrangements with other manufacturers, and the one-fifth scale model of the new bus was loaned to Leyland Motors in April.

The agreement allowed AEC and Park Royal to manufacture vehicles based on the new design, or incorporating features from it, but required that any vehicles sold to companies which were not associated with the British Transport Commission should have in their price an unspecified sum which would be paid back to LT in recognition of the high development costs of the vehicle.

AEC was easily the leading supplier of buses to London – an agreement in 1933 specified that AEC would supply at least 75 per cent of London's annual new bus requirements – but outside the capital it was a different story, and while AEC was still a major player, with significant customers as far north as Aberdeen and as far south as Torquay, outside London it was generally number two to Leyland.

London Transport was Britain's biggest bus buyer, and to win a share of its business Leyland had modified its Titan PD2 chassis to suit LT's needs, including the ability to accept a standard RT-style body. Thus was born the RTL. And it was Leyland rather than AEC which provided London's first 8ft-wide double deckers in the shape of the RTW class.

Leyland recognised the need to maintain its relationship with LT, and in the summer of 1954 Leyland's managing director, Henry Spurrier, wrote to stress the importance his company placed on LT's business saying, in relation to the new model being developed by LT: "We need the opportunity to develop and test to near perfection a type or types required for your purposes immediately".

Spurrier noted that the 2,000-plus Titans supplied to LT after the war had performed well but added "A development and proving period would undoubtedly have saved both your concern and our own quite a lot of expense in eliminating teething troubles". His point was that he wanted Leyland to be involved in the new Routemaster project from the start, and to build one or more prototypes. Leyland had just closed its body-building facility, so wasn't seeking to offer complete vehicles.

Spurrier concluded – a little piqued in tone, perhaps? – "Even at this late stage, we would welcome an opportunity to build one or more sets of Leyland units into a bus structure developed by LTE [and] we would be prepared to do our part of the work free of cost, submitting the completed buses to you for duration test in reasonable time, before you decide to place any bulk orders".

LT could see benefits in dual-sourcing, and in August 1954 the decision was made to build two more prototypes using Leyland units. These were to be supplied at a price of £4,500 which was roughly the price of two equivalent "normal type" chassis. Three other builders were seen as possible suppliers of the body, building to existing LT drawings. One was Weymann, which had built bodies for RTs. Another was ECW, chosen because it was, like LT, a subsidiary of the BTC. And the third – held in reserve in case ECW declined to get involved – was Saunders Roe.

While LT was developing the Routemaster, Leyland was in fact working on its own bus for the future, the innovative rear-engined Lowloader. By mounting the engine under the stairs and driving the rear axle, Leyland was able to reduce the height of the lower saloon gangway and thus the total height of the bus. Two Lowloader prototypes were built (one with a Saunders Roe body), and both entered service in 1954. Leyland initially offered to supply a Lowloader to LT to test, but in the end did not follow this through.

Those who criticise the Routemaster for its conventional layout overlook the fact that every double decker in service in the UK at the start of the 1950s had a front engine, and the vast majority had the entrance at the rear. So the Routemaster was, in layout, very much a product of its time.

However in construction it was breaking new ground. Most bus bodies at that time used a mixture of steel and timber in their construction. There were a few pioneers using aluminium, but steel framing would be commonplace on bus bodies until the 1970s when aluminium gradually gained ground – and steel is still the preferred material for bus bodies in many mainland European countries.

It was not just the use of aluminium, novel enough in itself at the time, which made the Routemaster unusual, but the use of integral construction. Indeed, it can be argued that by a number of criteria the Routemaster was the most successful integral double decker ever built in Britain. Leyland – working with MCW – had unveiled its Atlantean as an integral in 1956, but by the time production started in 1958 had decided to build a conventional chassis, in part to cut costs. AEC's Bridgemaster was an integral, but only 179 were built. It wasn't until the Leyland Titan of the late 1970s – designed for LT, of course – that an integral double-deck bus would achieve real volume production. Yet even the Titan – 1,159 production models built in seven years – achieved less than half the figure of the Routemaster.

When Bristol and ECW were nationalised they were restricted to supplying vehicles to other state-owned businesses – mainly the Tilling and Scottish Omnibuses groups. Body orders from the Tilling and the Scottish groups used most of ECW's capacity, but as new bus orders slowed down in the early 1950s Bristol had the capacity to build more chassis than both these organisations were ordering. It filled some of its excess capacity by building lorries for the nationalised British Road Services.

It's against this background – state ownership of LT and of Bristol, and a decline in demand for buses – that you have to see an approach by Bristol to LT in July 1955, in which it sought to get involved in the Routemaster project. Bristol had in fact been shown the Routemaster designs in 1953, although at that stage there was no suggestion that they should be involved. They were at that time finalising the design of the Lodekka, and working on designs for lorries for BRS.

The approach got a cool reception from LT for a number of reasons. For a start, one of the key requirements for the Routemaster was an engine of around 9.5 litres capacity and a semi-automatic gearbox. Bristol could not supply these (its AVW engine was an 8.2-litre unit) but what it did want to supply was 25 per cent of LT's requirement for "front and rear suspension units, etc" arguing that whichever manufacturer was awarded that work would be faced with the same tooling costs.

However at this stage LT was already working with Leyland on the supply of two prototypes and saw the Lancashire-based manufacturer as the second source of unit supplies. LT argued that if Leyland were to drop out, it would make more sense to procure all of the Routemaster units from AEC. There was also a moral argument in Leyland's favour over Bristol, with an LT memo in October 1955 stating "To transfer 25 per cent of the supply requirements from the Leyland Company ... would amount to a breach of faith. Leyland's design experience would be lost and London Transport would gain nothing in exchange."

In a letter from LT's Chief Mechanical Engineer (Road Services), A A M Durrant, to Bristol's General Manager, A W Hallpike, this is spelled out, with the comment: "We have examined the suggestion from every angle and our conclusions are that it would not be to the Executive's advantage either from the technical or the financial point of view to extend the number of contractors engaged in the manufacture of equipment."

Referring to Leyland's costs in producing running gear for two prototypes, Durrant went on to say: "It has now become clear that Leyland will be obliged to incur considerably more than the sum they will recover from us, on the design and development of the special equipment". He added that in the light of this Leyland would be given the opportunity to produce running gear for the Routemaster – provided it was commercially and technically acceptable to LT.

And that closed the chapter on Bristol's possible involvement.

By the summer of 1956 the Routemaster development programme was gathering pace, and LT had invited three manufacturers to tender for the body structure – Park Royal, ECW and Weymann. The tender had specified two batches, an initial 200 to be followed by a further 500, with production to reach a rate of 34 a month.

Park Royal was the cheapest, quoting £2,240 per vehicle for the first 200, and £2,173 for the subsequent 500. Next came ECW, which quoted £2,331 for the first 200 and £2,296 for the remainder. Weymann was the most expensive. Its figures were £2,550 and £2,455 respectively – some 14 per cent above Park Royal's prices.

Apart from being more expensive than Park Royal, ECW had another problem. Much of its capacity was committed to supplying the Tilling and Scottish groups, and mindful of this ECW said it could produce no more than 50 Routemaster structures a year – that's just over four a month against LT's stated requirement of 34 a month.

But ECW's involvement had been of commercial value. An internal LT memo of June 1956 notes: "The price quoted by Park Royal Vehicles is considered to be a very favourable one and fully reflects the competitive conditions under which these tenders have been sought, more particularly that provided by the ability of the Executive to secure a quotation from Eastern Coach Works".

In other words, mindful of ECW's relationship with LT as fellow subsidiaries of the British Transport Commission, Park Royal had submitted a keen price to try and secure what was a major contract. Park Royal wasn't to know that ECW had capacity constraints – and even if it did, it could have reasoned that ECW might have been willing to sacrifice some of its Scottish business to secure the LT work, as the BTC-owned Scottish Omnibuses group obtained the majority of its bodies from companies other than ECW.

The tender submissions were broken down to show material and labour costs, with the balance of the quoted price covering overheads and profit. LT noted that for the Routemaster, Park Royal's overheads and profit represented 56 per cent of its labour costs. This was a lower figure than either Weymann (59 per cent) or ECW (66 per cent) and, lending credence to LT's belief that the threat of competition from ECW had helped keep Park Royal's prices down, it was significantly lower than the figure of 77 per cent which had applied to the cheapest RT body contract placed with Park Royal.

At this stage LT was planning to order 1,540 Routemasters to replace 1,507 trolleybuses, and decided that in the interests of continued and uninterrupted production it should place an order for 700 vehicles on the terms set out by Park Royal, with an order for between 450 and 840 additional vehicles being negotiated on "the best terms obtainable" but in any event no higher than the figure quoted for the second 500. Park Royal agreed to this, subject to an allowance for rises and falls in its costs. AEC would supply 75 per cent of the running units – 1,155 sets, with Leyland supplying the balance of 385 "subject to satisfactory performance of the prototype supplied by them".

A comparison with the theoretical cost of a new RT was carried out. It was estimated that in 1956 an RT would have cost £5,380, compared with £5,750 for a Routemaster. This comparison made a number of points including the lower cost per seat for a Routemaster – £90 against £96 – and that around £200 of the extra cost was attributable to materials, and in particular the use of light alloy to save weight which would reduce the fuel bills.

A final justification for buying the Routemaster – and justification is certainly how LT's cost comparison reads – is that the total cost of 1,540 Routemasters for trolleybus replacement would be £8,855,000, whereas if 56-seat buses were used it would require 1,760 vehicles at a total cost of £9,469,000.

Although the initial Routemaster programme was geared directly to trolleybus replacement, it was intended that Routemasters would replace RTs too, and when it came to writing down the cost of the four prototypes – £185,000 – and of tooling for body and running units – another £185,000 – it was argued that this expenditure should be spread over 5,000 vehicles – 1,540 for trolleybus replacement and 3,460 of the rest.

With a theoretical operating life of 15–18 years, LT could, in 1956, quite reasonably expect to be replacing most of its 6,750 RTs (a figure which includes RTLs and RTWs) between 1961 and 1972 at a rate of around 500 a year on the basis of ten 64-seat Routemasters replacing eleven 56-seat RTs, but the figure of 5,000 was never reached.

Motor Bus v. Trolleybus

In 1953 the British Transport Commission asked London Transport to present it with the case for replacing trolleybuses with motor buses. The response included the possibility of some Routemaster trolleybuses.

When the LPTB decided in 1946 that the replacement of the remaining trams would be with the use of buses and not trolleybuses, it was felt that when the trolleybuses introduced between 1935 and 1940 became due for withdrawal, these too would probably be replaced by motor buses and not new trolleybuses. This course was in mind when the 70-seater bus committee was set up in 1949, which envisaged the possibility of up to 3,000 30ft long buses replacing not only trolleybuses but also buses of standard length on routes suitable for bigger vehicles. By 1950 it had been decided that no further 30ft long buses or trolleybuses with twin rear axles would be designed for London and that if the 30ft length was required, the Ministry would be asked to consider increasing the limit for two-axled double deckers, having already done so for single deckers in 1949. The second batch of Q1 trolleybuses, delivered in 1952, were the last of the line.

In 1953 the BTC requested a report from the London Transport Executive on the case for substituting buses for trolleybuses, particularly the financial and foreign exchange implications.

A draft report was drawn up and dated 27th May 1953. The structure of the new vehicle, it was stated, was such that it could be powered either by an oil engine or by electrical equipment. One option therefore was to use the same basic design in trolleybus form and then, when the time came to replace the RTs, a bus version. Both options assumed a two-axle vehicle within the then maximum permitted length of 27ft and seating 64 passengers. There was a possibility however that a trolleybus version would only be able to seat 62 because the roof-mounted equipment could require two fewer seats on the top deck to pass the tilt test.

London Transport may have been anxious not to appear to be presenting the BTC with a fait accompli, but by this time there could have been little enthusiasm at 55 Broadway for buying a new fleet of trolleybuses. The development from 1951 of what became the Routemaster had proceeded on the basis that it would be a motor bus. It stated in the report, however, that it would be possible to overhaul the new vehicle at its Aldenham works whether it were built as a bus or a trolleybus. Though not mentioned in the memorandum, plugging Aldenham into the trolleybus system would not have been difficult, the wiring for route 645 reaching within about a mile of it.

WITH the exception of a fleet of 127 postwar trolleybuses in the south-west suburbs, the London Transport trolleybuses are to be replaced by diesel buses of a new lightweight type, beginning in about three years' time. This decision has been made with the approval of the British Transport Commission, and after consultation with the Minister of Transport. There are 64 trolleybus services operated by 1,764 vehicles with 253 miles of route. They carry 750 million passengers a year, or one-fifth of London's road passengers.

All London trolleybuses, except those mentioned, will have completed their useful lives in a few years' time. They will by that time have served Londoners for about twenty-one years, each having run something like 900,000 miles in service. Thereafter, maintenance will be heavy and uneconomic, and replacement will become a necessity. It has been decided, after close study of all the factors involved, that the best vehicle for replacement will be the oil-engined bus—a vehicle which is already serving most of London.

The replacement of 70-seater trolleybuses by vehicles seating 64 had some implications for the number of vehicles needed. Allowing for a slight increase in passenger waiting times during the height of the peaks, the report claimed that only 33 additional 64-seaters would be needed to replace the 70-seaters. With the use of buses, economies in scheduling would be possible, such as the elimination of duplicate mileage where two types of vehicle run over the same stretch of route. The use of new trolleybuses assumed retention of the existing route structure, whereas with buses some merging of existing bus routes and former trolleybus routes would take place.

Concern had been expressed about the effect on foreign exchange of using oil instead of electricity. It may have been felt a little too risky to ask for unbiased advice on this matter but, whatever the motive, the question was referred to the Shell-Mex oil company. They made out a case for a net foreign exchange advantage in favour of using oil on the basis that the coal that would otherwise be used for electricity generation would be available for export. It was also suggested by Shell that the price of coal was likely to rise more than the price of oil, a suggestion that history was to prove incorrect.

The report then moved on to the question of the best vehicle for the job of providing the most efficient service for Londoners. The comparative rigidity of the trolleybus system was seen as a serious disadvantage when population changes occur and if traffic on existing routes declines it could be difficult to use the vehicles elsewhere. The inability of trolleybuses to overtake other trolleybuses meant that a heavily laden trolleybus running late holds back all following trolleybuses on the same road. At busy points on bus routes, more than one stop was provided, with the routes served being split between them, to reduce the size of queues. This was not possible with trolleybus routes, again because the vehicles needed to stay in 'fixed succession'. The delays caused by dewirements were also referred to.

Particular stress was given to the advantage of the bus over the trolleybus when it came to the routeing of services, pointing out that trolleybuses were not, and were never likely to be, allowed to run through the centre of London. The report listed the nine 'in-town' terminals, showing that nearly 7,000 trolleybus journeys terminated on the edge of central London each day on Mondays to Fridays. Two of these, however, were Shepherd's Bush and Hammersmith, natural traffic objectives in their own right. Top of the list was Aldgate, with 1,148 journeys per day. The successors to the busiest of the routes terminating here, the 653, have never to this day extended beyond Aldgate. The report accepted that most of the terminals would be retained whatever type of vehicle was operated, as congestion would prevent all of the routes being projected into the centre. It was also accepted that routes terminating on the edge of the central London area were less prone to delays. Nevertheless, it was felt that on traffic grounds 21 of the 56 trolleybus routes surveyed could be modified in some way to advantage.

Summarising the financial effects, the report stated that 64-seater trolleybuses would have working expenses roundly £26,000 per annum less than 64-seater oil buses, but that there were various factors that would affect this calculation. These included the risk that it might be possible to provide only 62 seats on the trolleybus, new expenditure that may be needed to maintain the electricity supply for 20 years or more and the value of the accommodation for additional buses at trolleybus depots converted to bus operation. Taking these factors into account it was felt by the Executive that there was little if any financial advantage in retaining trolleybus operation and that the better service it anticipated being possible with oil buses was being made possible without, in effect, having to pay a price for it. A memorandum to this effect was submitted by London Transport to the BTC on 17th July 1953. It asked for approval for replacement of all but the post-war trolleybuses by 64-seater oil buses. The official announcement of the changeover was made on 28th April 1954. The possibility of a Routemaster-style trolleybus, always slim, was now non-existent.

Left The April 1954 announcement of trolleybus replacement, as reported in the trade newspaper *Motor Transport*.

Naming the New Bus

The Chairman of London Transport was keen for the new bus to have a name that would help to publicise it. Routemaster was not the only name suggested, nor was it original. Correspondence in Transport for London's archives tells the story of the search for the name that was to become so well known.

When what was to become known as RM 1 was shown to representatives of the technical press at Chiswick in August 1954, no name had been decided for the new bus design. A technical press release dated 25th August 1954 simply refers to the vehicle as "London Transport's New Double-Deck Bus" with no hint of a name or type code. When interviewed later, Michael Robbins recalled that Durrant had suggested Roadmaster, a name "which the Board felt sounded rather bullying". By early September the name Routemaster had been proposed and on Tuesday 7th September Mr Stanley Madden, of the Secretary's office, phoned trade mark agents J Cleveland & Company of Chancery Lane to ask whether the name had already been registered by anyone else. They found some similar names, including 'Roadmaster', which had been registered in September 1950 by the Excelsior Motor Company Ltd, a motor cycle manufacturer, and in July 1953 by the Dayton Cycle Company Ltd of Park Royal for pedal cycles.

"We are of the opinion," wrote the agents on the same day, "that the word 'Roadmaster' is so near to the mark propounded that there would be every likelihood of confusion between the two and consequently we cannot recommend that you use or apply to register the word in question". The Equipment and Engineering Company Ltd (ECO) were already using the name Routemaster at this time for a range of destination indicator gears, but no mention is made in their advertising of the name having been registered by them as a trade mark so it would not have been known about by J Cleveland.

On the 7th September letter received by Mr Madden from the agents, he has written in pencil the word 'Ridemaster' – perhaps his own idea for a name – but two days after the date of the letter, 'Routemaster' was decided upon.

It was Michael Robbins's recollection that the classification RM may have been decided upon a little before the name was finalised and this is borne out by the fact that all the suggested names would be suitable for this type code.

The code RM was a logical choice for a bus that had earlier been referred to as the IM and later as the RT12. The last recorded reference to the code IM is in a memo dated 12th November 1953. On 14th November, a letter from P Lunghi, the Chief Draughtsman, used the term RT12 and this persisted until September 1954. On the 9th of that month, the day on which 'Routemaster' was decided on, Mr Lunghi wrote to Park Royal Vehicles about the "RT12 prototype vehicle – preparation for Commercial Motor Show".

On 13th September 1954 the name was made known to the trade press. On the same day Durrant wrote to Michael Robbins, Secretary to the Executive, asking if action could be taken to have the new name registered as a trade mark. In a press release to the national press dated Thursday 23rd September it was announced that the 'London Bus of the Future' going on display at the Commercial Motor Show the following day would be called the 'London Transport Routemaster'. It did not apparently at this stage feel sufficiently confident to use the name Routemaster on its own.

The integrally mounted (IM), or 'RT12', bus was completed at Chiswick on 3rd September 1954. This handwritten note, preserved in Transport for London's archives, provides us with the date on which the decision was made to use the name 'Routemaster'. It is signed by Percy Shaw-Scott, personal assistant to Durrant and addressed to Stanley Madden in Michael Robbins's office. Four days later the name for the new bus was made public in a press release.

Mr MADDEN.

ROUTEMASTER.

We go ahead with it, but as far as I am aware we don't do any registering at the present time. I have asked Mr Durrant to confirm with Mr Robbins.

Many Thanks

9/9/54.

The painted advert added to RM 1 for the Show.

LONDON TRANSPORT "ROUTEMASTER"

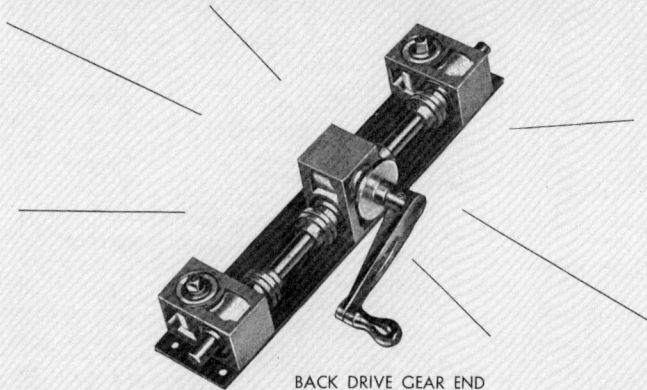

LONDON TRANSPORT
55 Broadway : S.W.1

13.9.54   TPN.1120

THE LONDON TRANSPORT "ROUTEMASTER"

The new double-deck bus, of which a prototype is to be shown at the Commercial Vehicle Exhibition at the end of the month (and which was inspected by representatives of the Technical press on August 25th), is to be known as the LONDON TRANSPORT ROUTEMASTER. It will carry the type letters "RM".

These type letters will not only be descriptive of the name given to the model but will also perpetuate the letter "R" which has been associated with London Transport's post-war vehicles of standardised design (i.e. RT, RTL, RTW, RLH, RF and RFW).

Since the occasion of the Technical press pre-view, measurements of actual weight and tilt angle of the prototype have been obtained. The all-up weight is 11 tons and the unladen weight is 6 tons 14 cwt. 2 qrs., as against the estimate of 6 tons 17 cwt. 2 qrs. given in TPN.1117, the original description of the vehicle.

A full 29° was obtained on the tilt test.

PRESS OFFICE
ABBey 1234 : Ext.70

The Executive, through its agents F J Cleveland, pursued the matter of registering the name 'The London Transport Routemaster' and British Trade Mark Application No. 734,141 was filed during the period of the Commercial Motor Show. The Registrar replied in January 1955 that the application was not valid because London Transport were not selling goods but providing a service. At the time a business had to be selling, or at least hiring, goods in order for a trade mark to be issued. Further correspondence on this matter continued until April 1956, when Michael Robbins wrote to the trade mark agents advising them that, as no objections had been received to London Transport's use of the name, the application was no longer to be proceeded with.

The suffix 'master' was something of a 'fifties fashion – at the 1954 show were vehicles named Hillmaster and Worldmaster and in other areas of manufacturing names such as Flightmaster, Shavemaster and Heatmaster were in use. When AEC launched its own integrally built double decker at the 1956 show, it was given the name Bridgemaster. Some at the 1954 show felt that the name Routemaster sounded rather American – Roadmaster was a Buick car model among other things – but today it sounds essentially British through association with the bus that became a legend.

Above left Although the name 'Routemaster' had not been registered by anyone, it was not original, having been in use since 1950 by the Equipment & Engineering Co. Ltd for a range of destination indicator gears. There is nothing to suggest, however, that the name was consciously copied by London Transport.

Above The press release to the trade magazines announcing the name.

RM 1 inside Earls Court for the 1954 Commercial Motor Show. The scale model that can be seen in the bottom left hand corner of the photograph is the original 1952 one with the destination altered to show the name.

The RM's Reception

RM 1 was exhibited at the Earls Court Commercial Motor Show between 24th September and 2nd October 1954. Gavin Booth has been looking at the trade press reviews that followed the event.

Two themes jump out from the pages of the transport trade press in 1954 – the quest for higher-capacity buses and the need to reduce weight to achieve this. This was the world that RM 1 was introduced into, and of course the Routemaster achieved both high capacity and low weight in what at first glance was a fairly conventional package.

Representatives of the trade press were taken to Chiswick Works in August 1954 to see RM 1 in advance of its appearance a few weeks later on the AEC stand at the 17th International Commercial Vehicle Exhibition at Earls Court from Friday 24th September until Saturday 2nd October. The press preview meant that the weekly and monthly magazines were able to devote considerable space to the new bus. The weekly *Motor Transport* describes the new bus in a slightly downbeat way in its 24th September show preview issue. The writer suggests that the Routemaster "may not attract the attention it deserves, because it looks to be just another London bus a little larger and more modern in appearance, but nothing more", but continues: "the not unfamiliar appearance obscures an ingenious form of integral construction, coil suspension, a modified transmission giving the driver two-pedal control and an arrangement by which the power unit at one end and the rear axle and suspension can be detached from the main structure and wheeled away for overhaul and replacement".

Passenger Transport devoted six pages to RM 1 in its Commercial Show preview, and *Bus & Coach* carried three pages plus fold-out detail drawings in its October 1954 Buyers' Guide issue, published to coincide with the show.

Both magazines prefaced detailed descriptions of the bus with some background to the model. P M A Thomas, technical editor of *Bus & Coach*, refers back to a paper delivered to the International Union of Public Transport congress in 1953 by A A M Durrant, which drew attention to the weight-saving advantages to be achieved from integral or chassisless construction. This method of building, he said, was particularly applicable to the double-deck bus. Durrant had also suggested that it was time to consider discarding traditional leaf-sprung suspension in favour of a method giving passengers a better ride and the vehicle greater stability. He had also discussed the pros and cons of fully-automatic and semi-automatic transmission to ease the driver's task without a detrimental effect on fuel consumption.

Against this background, P M A Thomas writes: "No one who took an intelligent interest in the paper ... will be altogether surprised at the prototype of the Executive's future double decker, which has been given the name Routemaster".

The articles in the trade press describe how Mr Durrant and his team had started with a clean sheet of paper, and with the combined help of AEC and Park Royal produced a 64-seat bus that was no heavier with a full load than a 56-seat RT.

Opposite One of the drawings included in the October 1954 edition of *Bus & Coach* magazine, showing the main structural features of the Routemaster.

CONSTRUCTIONAL DETAILS OF NEW DOUBLE-DECKER

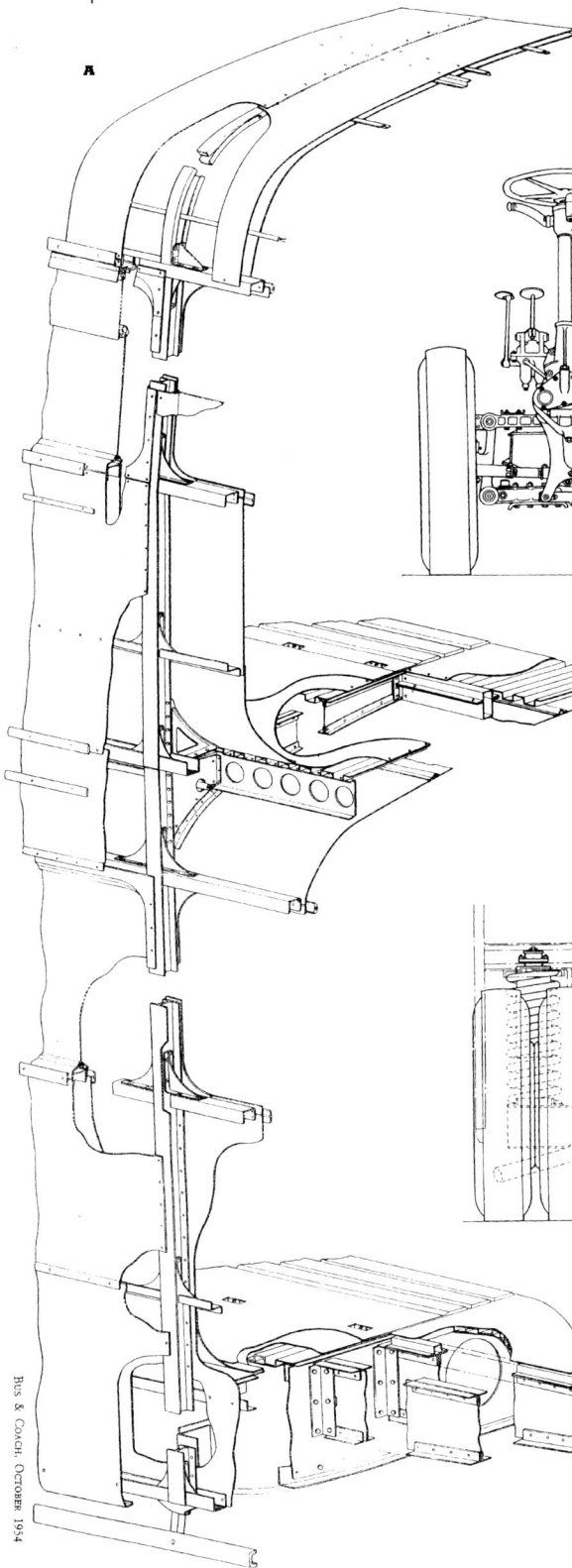

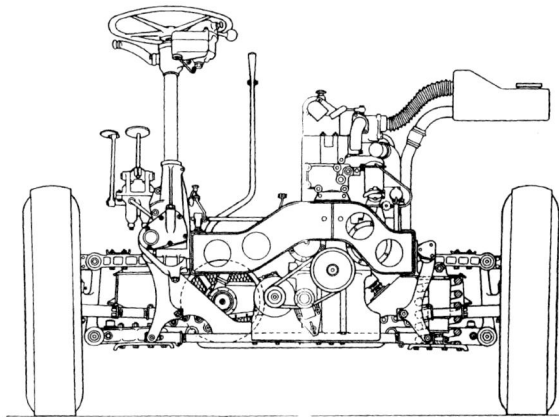

A Illustrating the main structural features of the light alloy integral body.

B A front elevation showing the methods by which the engine, the driving controls and the front suspension units are supported.

C A cross section through the engine mountings.

D Showing the rear axle and the rear suspension by helical springs and telescopic hydraulic dampers.

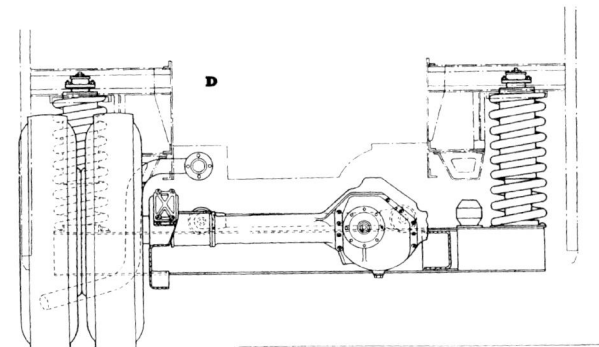

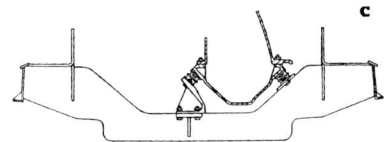

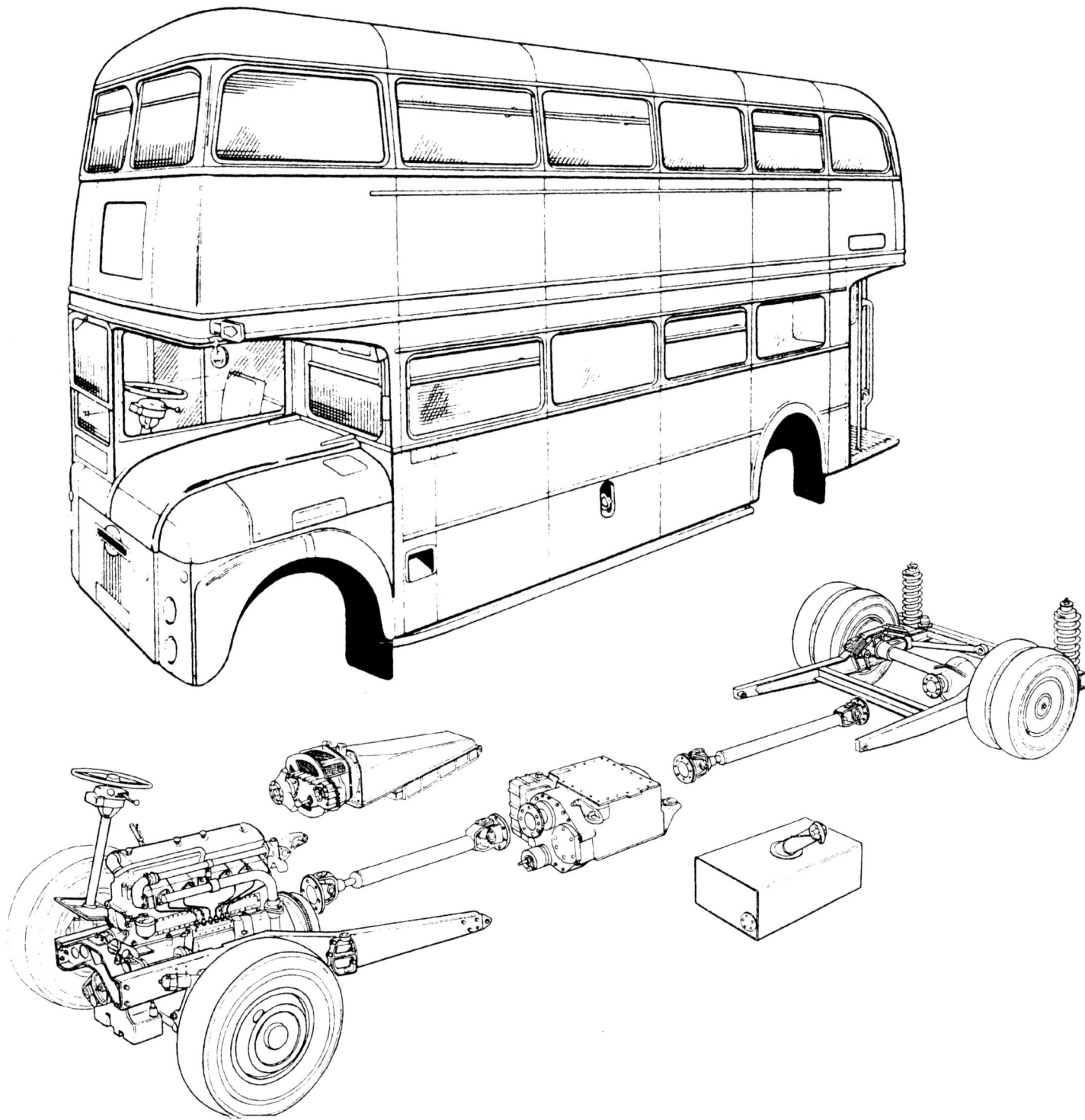

The anonymous writer in *Passenger Transport* refers to the history of the design: "Basic principles were tackled some six years ago when the postwar RT began to enter service. It is not the policy of London Transport to improve on a design so that batches differ and are non-standard. Instead, a design is chosen, proved and ordered, and as such enters service".

P M A Thomas was clearly impressed by the Routemaster in his *Bus & Coach* article, but recognised that London's needs were not necessarily those of the whole bus industry. "Whether this ambitious project will influence the future of bus design as a whole and as such mirrors the double-decker of the future only time can tell," he writes. "London Transport's problems, it has been argued in some quarters, are peculiar and so require peculiar treatment, the implication being that what satisfies the largest bus undertaking in the world does not necessarily suit the need of others." He concludes his article by congratulating all concerned with the design for their enterprise, and reveals that the estimated unladen weight of the complete bus was 6 tons 17½ cwt, but its actual weight was 3 cwt less – "an excellent achievement".

The Routemaster was one of the highlights of what was undoubtedly an important show, with a raft of new lightweight models making their debut, including the AEC Regent V and Leyland Titan PD2/20. And Leyland almost stole the show by sneaking its prototype rear-engined Lowloader, forerunner of the Atlantean, into the Earls Court demonstration park towards the end of the show.

The industry's reaction to the Routemaster makes fascinating reading. Edinburgh's transport manager, Moris Little, gave his impressions of the show in the November 1954 issue of *Bus & Coach*. He regarded RM 1 as "technically the most interesting exhibit" there, adding "it is curious that while one section of the [British Transport] Commission can exhibit through its association with a manufacturing company another section has no such avenue. The reference here is, of course, to the Bristol Lodekka, another vehicle of the now nationalised section showing considerable advance in technique. BTC companies are not, of course, the only ones showing advance. The Birmingham & Midland Motor Omnibus concern is also well out in the forefront, particularly in the matter of suspension arrangements, the use of plastics and general lightweight construction. Here again they are operators and not manufacturers for other users and so not within the ambit of Earls Court exhibition."

Moris Little pays tribute to those who designed the Routemaster "for facing up to the combined problems of increased capacity and comfort at a single stroke" and looks at the other high-capacity double-deckers that were also on show, including of course one of Edinburgh's now-legendary Metro-Cammell Orion-bodied Leyland Titan PD2/20s that managed to match the 64 seats of the Routemaster in a conventional bus weighing just less than RM 1 – though nobody would claim that the interior finish in one of his famous "monstrous masses of shivering tin" could ever compare favourably with the Routemaster.

Another industry leader writing in *Bus & Coach* was W J Crosland Taylor, general manager of the Crosville company. A fan of double deckers, he remarks that there were plenty at the show, "... and that is how it should be, for are they not the operators' best friends? They earn more per vehicle. Who can deny it? They cost very little more to run and they don't date for years and years."

Turning to the Routemaster, Mr Crosland Taylor describes how "I stood by the back step watching people get on and off, and could hardly believe my eyes. It was bouncing up and down – the back platform, I mean. I had not read about the coil springs before coming to the show, but they were very evident as soon as anybody walked about on either lower or upper deck". "The 64 seats were a useful number," he continues, "and cleverly placed. I wondered what it had cost, but dare not ask, though I remembered that LTE specifications were sometimes expensive to comply with."

Another commentary on the show in *Bus & Coach* came from industry veteran Arthur Twidle. He noted that the Routemaster adhered to "the old general concept of engine in front, but with the radiator underneath to increase passenger space, a step up from the platform to the lower saloon as before, and much the same overall height." He expresses concern about the move to increased seating capacity, suggesting that there could be problems collecting fares. "It has always seemed to me that a better line of approach would lie in devising means for more rapid loading and unloading. This, I feel, would result from the provision of a larger platform and a lower floor to the inside saloon, with no step." He cites the Bristol Lodekka and Leyland Lowloader as examples of what he describes as "low high-bridge" buses, and regrets that they were not on show in Earls Court for direct comparisons to be made.

The annual extra issue produced by *Bus & Coach* on 15th November 1954, titled 'British Design for 1955', allowed the editorial staff to compare the Routemaster with other new double deckers, notably the Bristol Lodekka and Leyland Lowloader. They argue for two-axle double deckers to be 30ft-long like single deckers, rather than the then current 27ft, suggesting that the double decker would receive a further boost from this, adding "There is no logical foundation for the existing length differential between the two classes of public service vehicles." In less than two years 30ft double deckers became legal, and this helped models like the Leyland Atlantean, although it would be some years before Routemaster production switched to longer buses.

The anonymous writer, probably P M A Thomas again, notes that the Routemaster had "emerged successfully from a series of searching tests at the Motor Industry Research Association's proving ground and elsewhere", but suggests that it is fair to regard it only as a prototype, in contrast to the Lodekka, which by then was in regular production. He notes that reducing height was not an issue with the Routemaster, and that London Transport's rather different aims have been attained "by discarding traditional design in several respects, though the appearance of the bus is not greatly changed, the half cab and the open rear platform being retained".

Correspondence in the trade newspaper *Modern Transport* was mostly focused on the limited destination display fitted to RM 1. A letter from Mr H T Eaton in the 2nd October issue led to three other letters being included in the 9th October edition, two of which gave a well reasoned defence of London Transport's initial decision.

MODERN TRANSPORT

LETTERS TO THE EDITOR

The New London Bus

SIR,—The new RM type of bus for London seems to incorporate many new features which, I am quite prepared to believe, will be of great benefit to the passenger and operating staff as well as proving economical. London Transport does not let the passenger down with its vehicles. But in designing a bus primarily for replacement of trolleybuses surely it has taken its terms of reference too much to heart in the matter of destination blinds. Surely a bus to work on erstwhile trolleybus routes does not have to continue with the inferior blinds that the trolleybus had? Indeed, if the prototype design goes unchanged, the space available for blinds will, apparently, be less than the present space on the London trolleybuses.

It is surely taking economy too far (and is a retrograde step) to do away with the present excellent, large and comprehensive destination indicators on the RT buses.—Yours faithfully,
H. T. EATON.
12 Chillerton Road, S.W.17.

LETTERS TO THE EDITOR

The New London Bus

THE MASTER TOUCH

SIR,—The letter from Mr. H. T. Eaton in MODERN TRANSPORT of October 2 concerning the destination blinds on the new L.T.E.-type RM bus is in complete contrast to my views. One of the basic pitfalls to be avoided in any design is that of showing contradictory information. This happens regularly on L.T.E. vehicles and is, in fact, inevitable when separate windows are used for the ultimate destination and places passed en route if a vehicle is liable at any time to take up a short working. That is, of course, assuming that bus crews cannot be persuaded to change the latter blind on such occasions even if they were provided with a separate description for each type of short working. Hence the recent abominable influx of the ambiguous and incorrect suffix "only" on London buses.

With the single window type, provided this is of sufficient size and full use is made of the available space (unlike the format employed on many L.T. trolleybus routes) enough space is available to display all the information required on the average route and no contradiction would occur on short workings since only those intermediate points applicable to the particular destination displayed would be indicated.

I endorse London Transport in its effort to break away from the RT style, thus eliminating a bad anomaly to the benefit of its passengers. Similarly, the strip type window to show only the ultimate destination over the platform entrance is quite sufficient for all normal requirements and once again avoids any contradictory information creeping in on short workings should the old style list of places en route have been retained. I do feel, however, that separate windows for route numbers at front and rear (and perhaps on the near side as well) would be an advantage.—Yours faithfully,
J. M. BARNES.
35 Horsell Park Close, Woking, Surrey.

SIR,—The new London RM type of bus may well be a great advance technically—but emphatically not so in the matter of destination blinds. The indicator over the platform (as on RT, RTL and RTW types) is an absolute necessity in London where no member of the public can possibly know the detailed route of each service. Is it too much to hope that London Transport will have second thoughts and retain the present admirable system?—Yours faithfully,
A. W. LEES.
58 Cavendish Road, N.4.

SIR,—Criticism by Mr. H. T. Eaton of the destination blind layout on the new RM bus of London Transport (MODERN TRANSPORT, October 2) emanates, I feel, from one interested primarily in design, as distinct from an ordinary member of the public.

The main concern, in my experience, of 95 per cent of London passengers is (a) the route number and (b) the ultimate destination which tells the traveller he is going in the right direction. Intermediate points are, to my mind, incidental, as the complete stranger will ask anyway, or consult the excellent route map issued by the L.T.E.

Six or seven points on a route blind mean very little on a long route such as the 27 for example, whilst at the other extreme the 117 blind has only three short names, Feltham, Ashford, Staines, amid a vast expanse of black; a complete waste of space.

By far the most useful blind in the RT layout is the one under the near-side canopy, and this has I believe been continued on the RM. The entire installation on an RT must mean a considerable amount of extra weight and expense, not to mention half a dozen or so additional lamps draining the battery. [Simplification of the blinds has saved 2½ cwt., or the equivalent of the weight of two passengers, on the RM type. Some guidance has, we understand, been obtained from a sampling of a passenger's opinions. — Editor, MODERN TRANSPORT.]

Reduction in blind displays interferes far less with the passenger, from a weight-saving point of view, than does the deletion of every opening window in the vehicle, a practice adopted by some operators, and leaving only two miserably small openings at the front, as a means of ventilation. One can only hope that this idea will not become widespread.—Yours faithfully,
J. TAYLOR.
46 Park Road, Hounslow, Middlesex.

Interestingly, the most critical comments on RM 1 came from the January-March 1955 issue of the enthusiasts' quarterly magazine *Buses Illustrated*. In an anonymous article 'Routemaster Reviewed', which we now know was written jointly by editor, E J Smith, and Alan Townsin, a regular contributor, the writers question the suggestion that the radiator was placed under the floor to shorten the bonnet in the interest of lower deck passenger space. The chief aim, they suggest, was to give access to the engine from the front which, they concede, is better for certain components; on the other hand they point out that "it is impossible to reach very far along the side of the engine from this position, and the nearside wing layout makes the neighbourhood of the injection pump even less accessible than is usual with full-width bonnet designs".

The writers wonder if London drivers will adapt to the two-pedal direct-acting transmission after preselective boxes, suggesting that placing the gear lever in the same position as on the RT "seems likely to lead to confusion, if not danger, should a driver used to [preselective boxes] attempt to preselect his gears in a moment of absent-mindedness".

The writers in *Buses Illustrated* are unimpressed by the looks of the Routemaster: "The design generally fails to reach the RT standard, still less show any improvement on it. Most obvious is the excessively upright frontal appearance". They hit out at the 'bulge' of the front panelling below the driver's windscreen: "Bulges of this type, however common on New Look double deckers owing their origins to the peculiar ideas of a well-known Midland municipality, are not what one expects from Chiswick, where the principle of a smooth, unbroken curve from cab front to roof was established 20 years ago with the STL5 body". Drawings are offered to show how the Routemaster could be modified to give a smoother front profile.

Like Mr Crosland Taylor, they criticise the number of rivets that are visible, as well as the lack of a 'turn-under' to the side panels, "resulting in a slab-sided appearance". The distinctive flashing indicator 'ears' are described as "ridiculous" and the writers wonder why they are not flush-fitting.

The distinctive design of RM 1's front end comes in for comment, too: "In the absence of a forward radiator, the seven chromium bars projected down from the front London Transport motif hardly seem in keeping with the aesthetic standards expected of the LTE, reminding one of transatlantic car designs. A plain mesh grille would be more functional". The reduced area of the destination indicators also comes in for comment.

A 1954 artist's impression of 'RM 51' in service.

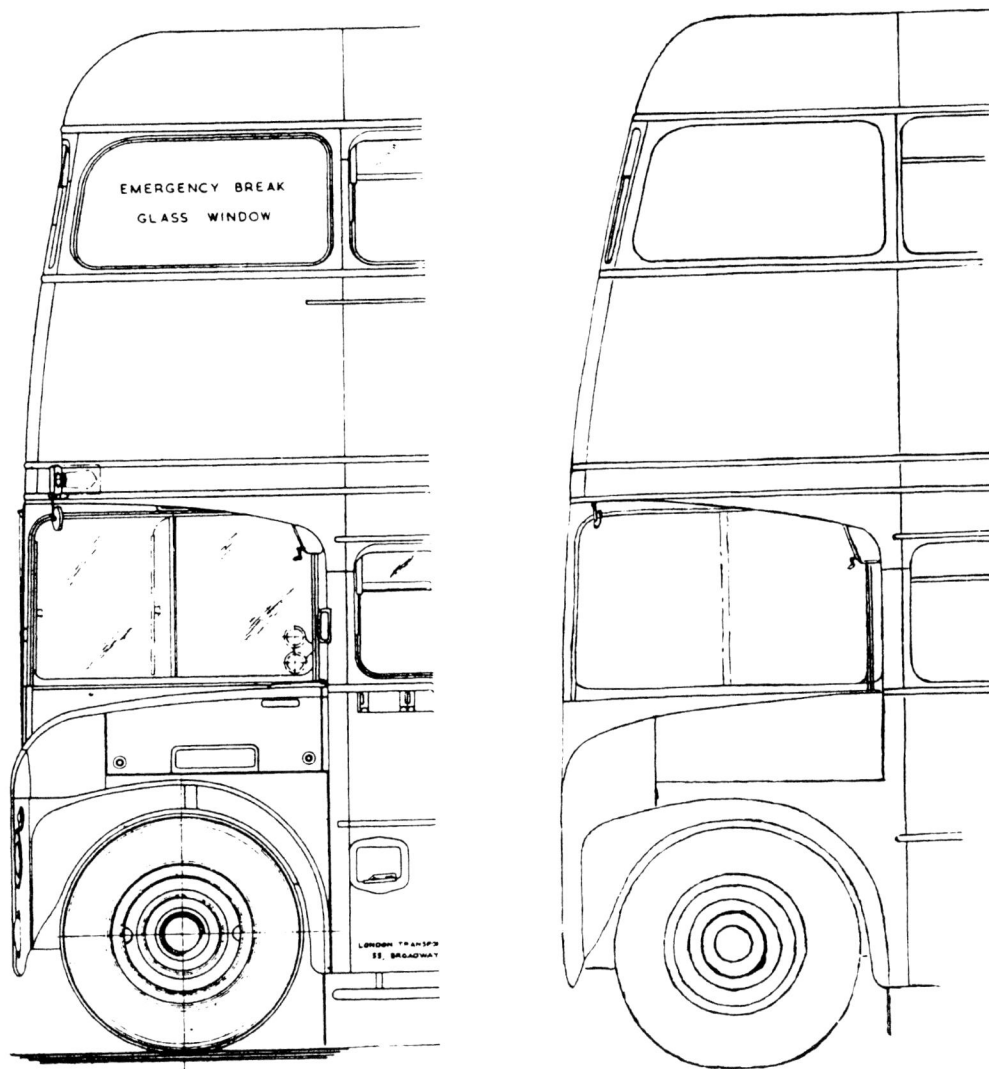

EMERGENCY BREAK
GLASS WINDOW

"To sum up," the *Buses Illustrated* writers conclude, "the RM forms a fascinating study. If this review seems severely critical in some respects, it is partly because an attempt to design a double-deck bus so free from the ties of preconceived ideas is worthy of careful and frank appraisal rather than hasty acceptance or outright condemnation. Further developments are awaited with interest".

Journalists who wrote for the weekly or monthly trade press in the 1950s confirm that the editorial policy was not to be too critical of the products of potential advertisers – while *Buses Illustrated* enjoyed more editorial freedom. Messrs Smith and Townsin both worked for AEC, which probably explains the anonymity – but they turned out to be very much on the ball with some of their criticisms of RM 1. The bus got a grille, though hardly in keeping with the smooth profile they advocated, and a much more comprehensive destination display was fitted. On the other hand, the indicator 'ears' stayed and it was not long before they ceased to look odd.

London Transport may not have got everything right first time round, but they certainly set the industry talking in 1954.

Developments in 1955

During 1955 the second prototype was completed and a number of modifications were made to RM 1. In addition two further prototypes were ordered, both with Leyland mechanical units and each with different bodywork. Extensive performance tests of RMs 1 and 2 took place at two testing grounds.

At the start of 1955, RM 1 remained the only Routemaster to be completed. It was joined on 8th February 1955 by RM 2. During the year both vehicles were subjected to extensive testing and neither entered passenger service before the year end, though both had clocked up mileages of around 10,000 by then.

The Country Bus department had been concerned about the unsuitability of RTs for the Romford Road Green Line services ever since they had been allocated to replace utility Daimlers in 1950 following the failure of the RTC project. In January 1955, Country Bus Operating Manager Geoffrey Fernyhough had asked the Board to consider hiring "one of the Southdown double-deck buses fitted with rear doors and heaters" for trial use on Green Line work. Durrant pointed out that these buses were not entirely suitable for Green Line work owing to their riding qualities and lack of luggage space. The same could be said for the RTs, the main criticisms of these being the standard bus seating and suspension and the sway experienced in the RT on cornering. At least the Southdown buses swayed less and had platform doors.

In January 1955 in response to Fernyhough's request, Durrant suggested that one of the second two prototype RMs could be suitably altered for trials as a double-deck coach with rear doors and heaters. He also suggested the replacement of the rear longitudinal seats downstairs by luggage pens, reducing the seating capacity to 56 but answering the luggage problem. Fernyhough was pleased to accept this suggestion. The purchase of two sets of running units from Leyland and one body each from Weymann and ECW was confirmed on 5th May 1955 and these became red RML 3 and Green Line coach CRL 4 in 1957.

The decision taken in 1952 to replace the RT style destination display by a single blind at front and back and a shallow blind above the platform had been taken as part of the drive to bring down the weight of the new bus as much as possible. London double deckers had been running around with wartime restricted destination displays for about ten years without too much apparent inconvenience to passengers and the full single-deck bus display was accommodated on one blind front and rear. By early 1955 second thoughts were being entertained about the Routemaster's destination display and a mock-up was prepared of a three-piece display for the front which became the adopted layout. It differed from the RT layout in having a shallower via blind box and in having the route number on the offside of the display rather than the nearside. The size and arrangement of blinds as used on the production RMs was decided on during the summer and the revised destination equipment for RMs 1 and 2 was ordered from the manufacturers in August 1955. The reason for moving the route number in the front display from the right hand side, where it was of more use in cases where part of an approaching bus was obscured by another bus or other traffic, to the left is not known. It may have felt to be more aesthetically pleasing.

On 27th January 1955 Brian Harbour, who had been appointed a Member of the Executive in October 1954, raised the matter of the destination displays to be provided on the new buses. Durrant replied that any review of the displays would best await the outcome of the investigations into the fitting of a heating system. This March 1955 photograph of RM 1 shows, in addition to a mock-up of the enlarged destination display, the anticipated space needed for the heater intake. The intake looks rather neater than the one in due course fitted to RM 1. The positioning of the route number on the left side of the main display was later to cause adverse comment from London Transport's chairman John Elliot when Lord Latham showed him a photo of RM 1 on the cover of the March 1957 *London Transport Magazine*. Previously the route number had been positioned on the right to be of more use to prospective passengers.

During its later operation, after its front end and radiator were altered, it ran on route 260 which passed my office and I saw a lot of it. Unfortunately, the reason I saw it so often was that it was frequently parked, bonnet open, in some sort of trouble outside the garage. The Cricklewood engineers would shake their heads in time-honoured fashion and opine that it would never be as good as the RT and that it would not last as long and that it was too sophisticated. Crews waiting to pick up their passing buses, none of whom had probably experienced the Routemaster in service, would look on with some amusement and join in the comments about its lack of durability. Nine years earlier I had talked to drivers on the new 3RT3s who had firmly attested that the RT would never be as good as the trusty old ST and LTs and would fall apart long before they reached the ripe old age of eighteen to twenty-one achieved by their forebears.

I managed to get at least one ride on each of the prototypes and can claim to be one of those rare people who managed to get down to Surrey on a day when RM 2 was not laid up with gearbox trouble and actually ran in service on the 406. I remember being less impressed by its performance on Reigate Hill, which seemed to be almost as much of a struggle as I recall experiencing on STs ten or more years earlier. That may have been because of the driver's lack of experience with the gearbox. Otherwise its qualities were hardly put to the test on such a relatively quiet and easy route but even at that early time, I recall being impressed by its stability when cornering. The coach version, CRL 4 as it was then known, was a revelation to me. I had never been a fan of the Leyland version of the RT because it was noisy and could be very rough when idling, but Leyland's version of the Routemaster was as smooth as silk and, if anything, slightly quieter than AEC's. I was quickly convinced that such a good riding, smooth and stable vehicle would be ideal for Green Line work, especially as it had real cushions of the deeper type used on coaches, and gave a then unrivalled quality of ride for the passenger. Unfortunately, later RMs fitted with Leyland engines seemed to repeat the mistakes of the RTL and did not live up to the wholly Leyland RML 3.

When the production Routemaster appeared at the 1958 Commercial Motor Show, it looked rather forlorn and out of date compared with the array of new models being shown for the 'provincial' market but we Londoners, for the most part, still had faith in a purpose-designed product. We had been promised a newly designed front end to replace the series of unattractive compromises fitted to the four prototypes but when I saw RM 8 I was more than a little disappointed. No attempt had been made to rethink the design of the front end, only of the bonnet and grille and to my eyes the resulting snout was, and remains to this day (despite several attempts at cosmetic improvement), ugly and out of place. The interior was brighter than on RM 1, with Chinese green (grey) panels on the window pillars but these were plastic and, looked even more cheap and cheerful.

When the first production Routemasters began to go into service during 1959, I was eager to sample the 'tried and tested' new product and get some real experience of the finished design with its fully-automatic gearbox. I was immediately introduced to one of the least endearing features of these early versions, the sickening jerk which accompanied nearly every gear change. It was reminiscent in some ways of a preselector in the hands (feet?) of a heavy-footed driver, except that in this case there was little that drivers could do to improve matters. Add to that the discomfort of the hard seats, on which the foam filling quickly collapsed to give little or no support and the stories we were hearing about all sorts of mechanical and steering faults and you can understand that I and many others began to think that we had a disaster on our hands. The problem of the jerk was ultimately solved with what was called the 'pause mechanism' which introduced a delay to the change. I can remember Mr Durrant (the legendary Chief Mechanical Engineer) explaining the technicalities of this to a very sceptical Deputy Chairman (Arthur Grainger). When the first buses were modified, I was able to discover for myself that Mr Grainger's scepticism was well founded. It took some time to put right.

CRL 4 at Chiswick in 1957 prior to entering service, a magnificent vehicle that proved to be the only Routemaster bodied by Eastern Coach Works. When the RM was launched in 1954 ECW had a record low order book. Only 599 bodies were built at the Lowestoft factory that year, compared with a record high of 1,062 in 1948. By 1956 there had been some recovery with a figure of 701, but the maximum of 50 bodies the company said it could produce for London Transport ruled it out of consideration for the bus version.

Passenger Comments

Inside RM 1 were posters asking members of the travelling public to write to London Transport's Public Relations Officer with their comments on the bus. Quite a number did and the PRO drew up a summary of compliments and criticisms for presentation to the Executive.

Just over a week before entering service, RM 1 was shown to newspaper journalists on the morning of Tuesday 31st January 1956. The invited guests were taken on a tour of the West End. "In difficult traffic conditions, with wet, greasy roads, RM 1 gave an impressive performance," wrote the reporter from the London 'Star'. It was driven by Mr Edwin Uwins from Reigate, probably one of the senior Green Line men there.

The bus entered passenger service on Wednesday 8th February and passengers were invited to send comments on RM 1 to the Public Relations Office at 55 Broadway. Between its first day in service and 21st April, 61 letters were received containing a total of 151 comments. Of these, 76 were criticisms of one sort or another, while 75 favourable remarks were recorded. The erratic heating and ventilating system no doubt led to the fact that ventilation was one of the items at the top of the list of criticisms, though some of the correspondents may have been unhappy about the lack of front opening windows. Seating comfort also gave rise to a lot of unfavourable remarks; plastic foam was used in order to contribute to weight saving. While there were 15 letters of praise for RM 1's suspension, there were also five letters of criticism, which may indicate different expectations or perhaps different qualities of driving. The transmission was another area where some passengers wrote approvingly and others disapprovingly, three commenting on its quietness and nine on its lack of it; vibration from the engine was also commented on. No-one praised the gearchanging on RM 1 and five people criticised it, which suggests that the semi-automatic gearbox compared unfavourably with the preselective gearbox in the RT types. Problems with the smoothness of gear changing were to continue into the first few years of production RM running until its fully automatic gearbox was perfected.

Despite the trouble London Transport had taken to enlarge the destination display on RM 1, six people criticised the arrangement and only one praised it. The general appearance of the bus received the most favourable comments, 30% of those writing in making appreciative comments and just 3% criticising it. Individual suggestions for improvements included the fitting of fluorescent lighting and a loudspeaker system to announce the stopping places.

Two letters highly praising RM 1 survive from November 1957. Mr S S Akeris, writing from Clifton Court NW8, congratulates the Board on what he refers to as the 'Forerunner Bus' (see wording on poster opposite). He comments on its spacious, neat, pleasant and warm atmosphere and smooth running. Mr Y Benstead from West Hampstead gets the name right and is complimentary about the omission of opening windows at the front and the shallower drop to the side windows, which would prevent a child putting its head out while travelling. He also praises the width of the gangway, the comfortable seating, the heating and the staircase.

By April 1956, RM 1 had received painted exterior advertisements all round. Colin Curtis recalls that this was the Chairman's idea; the engineers would have preferred not to have made a big show of it in case the bus broke down on the road.

One of the posters inside RM 1 inviting passengers to write in with comments.

THIS BUS is the forerunner of the future London bus and is on trial to test its general performance and suitability.

It is of lightweight construction, embodying special features contributing to your riding comfort.

If you would like to make any comments on the 'Routemaster,' please send them to the Public Relations Officer, 55 Broadway, S.W.1.

In the Country

London Transport's Country Bus Operating Manager Geoffrey Fernyhough felt that the Routemaster was not suitable for his area and wanted something different, preferably a bus specially designed to suit the different characteristics of Country Bus operations.

A few months before RM 2 entered service in the Country Area, the Operating Manager Geoffrey Fernyhough proposed to Durrant that a smaller-capacity and more austere double-deck bus be developed for use in his area, instead of the Routemaster. Having in the recent past eliminated almost all variety in the double deck bus fleet, London Transport at this time had a keenness for standardisation that verged on the obsessive. The Routemaster had been developed on a one size fits all basis and the newly opened overhaul works at Aldenham were designed to deal with a standardised fleet. If the case for a special vehicle could be made, however, Durrant describes its possible main features: a smaller engine with possibly a friction clutch and synchromesh gearbox; similar sub-frames to the Routemaster, including independent suspension, but with a specially designed body, possibly of lightweight steel, plainer than the Routemaster and seating 56 as specified by Fernyhough. As mentioned earlier the potential economies from a higher seating capacity enabling reductions in the number of buses were far fewer in the Country Area and so Fernyhough saw no need to have a capacity greater than that of the RT. Mr L C Hawkins, Executive member responsible for Finance, expressed interest in the ideas put forward following the discussions between Fernyhough and Durrant but said that he had in mind the possibility that RT vehicles could be retained in the Country Area until about 1970. Deliveries of RTs had only recently been completed and there were still a number of brand new buses in store because falling demand had rendered them surplus. Until the late 1960s, Hawkins envisaged a Country Bus double deck fleet (excluding low-bridge buses) all of the RT type. Only then would a replacement vehicle be needed.

Brian Harbour pointed out that there were also a number of routes in the Central Area where the type of double decker being proposed for the Country Area might be used. He considered it was commercially unsound for the green buses to be made up of out-of-date vehicles while all the modernisation was concentrated on the Central Area. The Deputy Chairman agreed. There was also the consideration that the Tilling and BET companies that met London Transport routes on the fringe of the Country Area were being modernised and would, like the RMs that met the green buses further in, increasingly show up the RT as outdated.

A special committee was set up to consider the possibility of a special vehicle – sometimes referred to as the 'provincial type' bus, which at 55 Broadway and Chiswick was a slightly derogatory term. London Transport felt that it always did things better. There was a lot to support this view at the time.

The committee first met on 7th August 1957, about the time RM 2 had been sent packing by the Country Bus department for its poor performance. The notes of this meeting indicate that the Bristol Lodekka was to be compared at Chobham testing ground with an RT in respect of fuel consumption. One of the arguments for introducing a new bus type to the Country Area would be possible fuel savings over the RT. No such tests appear to have taken place, however.

The matter of a special bus for the Country Area was raised at Durrant's meeting on a number of occasions in 1958 and 1959, but no justification could be found for buying a new 56-seater when enough RTs were available and would remain suitable for about ten years. In December 1958 Fernyhough sent a memo to Durrant about the lack of new buses in the Country Area when the replacement of RTs in the Central Area was due to start in 1962. Fernyhough argued that this would give rise to unfavourable comparisons in the minds of passengers and staff. Of particular concern was the fact that no heaters were fitted to RTs whereas these were becoming increasingly common on new buses, including of course the RM. Durrant responded by stating that heaters could be fitted to Country RTs at a cost of about £100 per bus; this modification was agreed in 1960 and carried out between 1961 and 1963.

In March 1960, Durrant reported that Fernyhough wanted a front entrance bus with doors when the time came to order new buses for his area. A new design of bus was in course of preparation by AEC which seemed likely to meet his requirements, Durrant stated, referring to the Renown.

A memo from Fernyhough to Central Bus Operating Manager Fred Lloyd and dated 17th August 1962 states his intention to have a batch of "33 front entrance RML vehicles" for trial operation from Northfleet garage. RMF 1254 had recently been delivered and after a short period on at least two Central Bus routes it had been intended that, early in 1963, the bus would be tried out in the Country Area. We will return to this subject in the chapter on Union Matters, but the August 1962 memo is the first written record of a desire by Fernyhough to have some Routemasters.

In February 1963 the Country Bus department received an AEC Renown front-entrance double decker, 8071 ML. It had been planned to operate this in comparative trials with RMF 1254, but this was not to be. It seems unlikely that Country Bus staff would have refused to operate the bus alongside 8071 ML, but as the RMF had been rejected by the union for the Central Area, it might have been seen as provocative to attempt its introduction at Northfleet. Of similar dimensions to the RMF, the Renown seated 76 passengers, 20 more than Fernyhough had said were needed in 1957 (the RMF seated 69). The Renown, like its poor-selling predecessor the Bridgemaster, was an AEC answer to the successful Bristol Lodekka, which the engineers had decided against for the Country Area. 8071 ML ran for four months on route 480 but failed to convince London Transport that there would be any advantage to it over the Routemaster and, soon after, 100 RMLs with semi-automatic transmission were ordered for the Country Area.

In July 1964, authority was given by the London Transport Board for the purchase of eight Daimler Fleetline double deckers for the Country Area. These were bought for an experiment into the economies that might result from running front entrance buses as two-man vehicles in the busy periods and, by shutting off the top deck, as one-man operated 'single-deckers' at other times. One-man operation of double deckers was prohibited at the time, and the novel idea of shutting off the top deck for one-man operation required an amendment to the rules to permit it. The aim was to enable savings in staff costs on routes unsuitable for full one-man operation with single deckers. The busiest routes would still have needed something like the Routemaster. Fernyhough's stated preference for RMFs was not followed, but Durrant indicated that FRMs could be available for the Country Area from 1967.

The intention for the RMLs was that 30 of them would replace RTs on a one-for-one basis on "two high-earning routes" and 70 would be allocated to nine high-frequency but unprofitable routes in place of 81 RTs. Of the routes that received RMLs, only the 347 had no reduction, while another big earner, the 480, reduced by just one bus from 18 to 17. The total number of RTs replaced by the 100 RMLs was 110 and some routes suffered substantial reductions in frequency, notably the 363 (from 8 buses to 6) and the 446 group (from 8 buses to 5).

Prototypes to Production

By 1956, the anticipated start of RM production had slipped from summer 1957 to summer 1958. The programme was to be further delayed, chiefly because of labour troubles at the Park Royal factory in which London Transport had entrusted all the body production, and the first production buses did not enter service until mid-1959.

With the prototype Routemaster in service, the engineers at Chiswick could begin to use information provided by its service running to incorporate necessary changes in the production version.

The matter of who would build the Routemaster fleet has been discussed in the chapter on Other Interests. On the same day that RM 1 entered service, 8th February 1956, a meeting was held at the Tilling Group's offices at 10 Fleet Street between Brian Harbour, Anthony Bull, A A M Durrant and Eric Ottaway of LTE and Stanley Kennedy, Chairman of the Tilling Group, J S Gavin, a member of the boards of both Eastern Coach Works and Eastern National, and Ralph Sugden, Director and General Manager of Eastern Coach Works, to discuss the possible involvement of ECW.

At the meeting it was stated that about 180 Routemasters would be needed by the end of 1958 to enable the first stage of the trolleybus conversion to take place in January 1959. A rate of production of 500 per year would be required. It was pointed out to ECW that London Transport felt it desirable for the production of Routemaster bodies to take place at one factory to enable the bodies to be produced economically and to the standards of interchangeability required by London Transport's maintenance procedures. Mr Kennedy questioned the wisdom of this on commercial and guarantee of supply grounds. He had told London Transport the previous November that his company would be able to supply the 500 bodies per year required by turning away some of its other business, but he now accepted that this was unrealistic. J S Gavin said the number ECW could produce was just 50 a year and asked if the planned Routemaster coaches could be built at Lowestoft.

For its part, London Transport was keen to obtain a quotation from Eastern Coach Works to make sure that the quotation it received from Park Royal Vehicles was competitive. Accordingly the Executive asked ECW to submit a tender for the whole or part of the quantity of RM bodies needed, irrespective of whether they would be in a position to manufacture them. Mr Kennedy agreed that ECW would be prepared to do this.

Although the number of RMs needed for trolleybus replacement was decided in 1956, the number that would later be needed for the replacement of RTs was still in question. There was also the matter of the Romford Road Green Line routes. It was suggested by Durrant in a memo dated 28th February 1956 that 50 RM vehicles could be available by July 1958 to replace the RTs on the coach service from Grays and Romford garages, the figure suggesting that he may have had ECW in mind as the likely builder. With ECW's prototype Green Line coach Routemaster expected in mid-1957, the date of July 1958 would give them the year they would need to build another 50. Fernyhough, the Country Bus General Manager, replied that 57 would be needed, plus a further three if summer only route 726 to Whipsnade Zoo were converted also.

This was, however, a time of falling passenger numbers and concern was expressed that there would be no work for the RTs displaced by the RM coaches. When, in June 1956, London Transport applied to the British Transport Commission for approval to purchase RMs to replace trolleybuses, no mention was made of the replacement of any Green Line vehicles. The authority given by the BTC in August was for 1,520 buses to be ordered, slightly fewer than the number then estimated as being needed for trolleybus replacement. The urgency of replacing the trolleybuses from 1959 onwards meant that, in accepting London Transport's argument that a specially designed bus was needed for London, the BTC had little choice but to give the go-ahead for this large number of vehicles of an as-yet unproven design. There was nothing else on the table.

The discussions leading to the ordering in May 1955 of running units and bodywork for two further prototype Routemasters have been covered earlier in this book. The first of the two to be taken into stock was the Green Line coach, classified CRL 4, which was collected in June 1957 from ECW's Lowestoft works by John Lewis of Chiswick works. His first impression was of an outstanding vehicle and he remembers the ECW works manager telling him that they wanted another order. They could certainly have coped with the RMCs and RCLs but could probably not have competed on price. John Lewis shared the driving back to London with ECW's delivery driver, but his main purpose for travelling back with the vehicle was to be an observer, checking its riding qualities and noise levels upstairs and down. His initial highly favourable impression was confirmed by the ride.

Following the approval from the BTC for the purchase of 1,520 Routemasters for trolleybus replacement, concern was raised within London Transport about the health issues that could be raised when or before the bus order was made public. Some concerns had already been expressed when it had been announced in 1954 that buses would replace the trolleybuses when the latter became due for withdrawal, but in 1955 cigarette smoking had for the first time been shown to be directly linked with cancer and there was now a greater concern about carcinogenic substances in the atmosphere. Public Relations Officer R M Robbins prepared a draft statement, for use if necessary, on the health issues connected with the Routemaster bus order early in September 1956. He wrote to Assistant Secretary J D C Churchill on 7 September 1956 with a copy of the suggested statement. It refers to research work carried out by the Medical Research Council which found that the diesel engine when well maintained "does not emit any harmful amount of substances liable to be injurious to health". The research was carried out for LT by three members of an MRC research group at a London Transport bus garage and the street outside. The public announcement of the order for 1,520 RMs was delayed until 28th September to coincide with the appearance of an article in the British Medical Journal which gave details of the Group's findings, to which the London Transport press release referred.

A redesign of the bonnet and wing arrangement was found to be necessary early in RM 1's service life. The design with which it entered service gave insufficient ventilation to the brakes, leading to excessive front brake temperatures and consequent shorter life for the brake linings. After seven months in service, RM 1 was sent to Chiswick in August 1956 to receive a number of modifications, the most visible being the moving of the radiator from under the engine to the front. Power assisted steering was also added, a feature later incorporated in RM 2 and RML 3, though not CRL 4 which was to be the only Routemaster never to have it. RM 1 re-entered passenger service in March 1957.

The matter of power assisted steering was under debate while the RM was being developed. RM 1 had proved heavier to steer than an RT and so in this respect was inferior from the driver's point of view. Other advances had benefited the driver, such as automatic gear changing and the reduced foot pressure needed by hydraulic braking. Durrant reported to the Board in 1956 that, subject to satisfactory tests, he strongly recommended the adoption of power assisted steering in the production Routemasters.

RM 1 made three special appearances in 1955 and 1956, the first being at an exhibition on the South Bank at Waterloo in June 1955 to commemorate the centenary of the discovery of aluminium. In 1956 the centenary of the LGOC was marked with a parade of buses in Regent's Park on 16th July. The man with the bowler hat and umbrella is Sir John Elliott, Chairman of London Transport. Later that year RM 1 appeared in the Lord Mayor's Show in November

Further work on the front end design was done by Douglas Scott for the second two prototypes. His idea, above, was tried out by modifying the existing one-fifth scale model, above right and right. Subtly different bonnets, using fibreglass, were tried out on RML 3 at Weymann's Addlestone factory and the design was used on this and CRL 4.

Scott-Ashford Associates May '56

In May 1956, Douglas Scott completed drawings with two alternative designs for the front end of the production RMs. This one formed the basis of the design adopted but had to be modified to accommodate the power steering header tank. The loss of the smooth curve always jarred with Douglas Scott, as mentioned earlier in the book.

The second alternative was much more radical, with the driver's windscreen sloping inwards from top to bottom and the radiator and lamp arrangement below the cab having a squashed oval appearance. This design was very much of its time and would have dated more quickly than the design chosen.

Scott-Ashford Associates May '58

RM 2's official completion date was 8th February 1955, but it was to be another 2¼ years before it entered service. At the end of 1955, Durrant was quoting May 1956 as the probable date by which RM 2 would be ready to start work on the 721. One of the factors which delayed its entry into service was the decision to change the gearbox from semi-automatic to fully automatic. A meeting was held at Chiswick on 8th May 1956 at which it was agreed that automatic transmission would be fitted to RM 2 and RM 3 (as it was then known) following the trial use since January of the AEC Monocoach equipped with this. In October, the semi-automatic gearbox originally fitted to RM 2 was used to replace the one in RM 1 and RM 2 received a fully automatic box. RM 2 suffered problems with its gearbox and it needed replacement twice within the following seven months, the second occasion being just four days after entering passenger service at Reigate. This garage had been chosen in March 1957, instead of route 721, partly because its drivers had become familiar with the automatic transmission on the Monocoach, which was returned to AEC in May about the same time RM 2 entered service.

The two Leyland prototypes appear to have had less serious mechanical problems in service, benefiting to some extent from experience with RMs 1 and 2. They shared excessive brake lining wear and short life of fan and dynamo belts and each suffered a few other minor problems, providing useful experience in the process. RM 3 was at an advanced stage of completion in spring 1956 and spent quite a lot of time in Leyland's experimental department and on test before delivery to London Transport from Weymann in summer 1957. Now numbered RML 3, the bus was fitted with power assisted steering in July 1957 and fully automatic transmission in October. It entered service in January 1958. One year after entering service the bus suffered serious collision damage but, although there had been problems with the brake linings, neither the bus nor the driver was found to be at fault.

CRL 4 had arrived a few weeks before RML 3 and started work in October 1957. The following year the coach and RM 2 were fitted with air suspension which, although causing some problems, proved of sufficient interest for London Transport to specify, as a further trial, air suspension on 50 RMs in 1959. CRL 4 also pioneered the use of an AEC air-operated gearbox instead of the hydraulic box fitted to the first three Routemasters, which was not ready to be put into production.

RM 2 was the first bus to be equipped with a fully automatic gearbox and power assisted steering, adding to the advances that RM 1 could boast. These new features played a large part in the long delay that occurred in RM 2's entry into passenger service. As outlined in the previous chapter, there was no intention of allocating RMs to Country Bus routes as long as the RT continued to be adequate but it was probably felt important not to ignore the Country Area completely and no doubt it was felt desirable to check that the RM would be suitable for all parts of London Transport's operations. The problems with the bus in service – for example it needed a new gearbox just four days after starting work – could not have improved Fernyhough's view of the Routemaster and, after just 2½ months, RM 2 left his department, never to return. Like RM 1, RM 2 received painted adverts publicising itself as London's bus of the future. These were covered over with ordinary commercial advertising before, or very soon after, entry into service. They were exposed again when the bus was repainted red, looking a little odd because the bullseye logos were in dark blue and Lincoln green. The posed photo of RM 2 is a coloured version of a black and white original in the LT Museum collection. It is dated June 1957; in August the bus was permanently withdrawn from Country Area service.

In Central Area service, RM 2 was allocated to Turnham Green garage, conveniently close to Chiswick Works. It ran on route 91 on Mondays to Saturdays and route 27 on Sundays. The first and second designs of Routemaster adverts were hand painted. The second design, shown here, was applied between 29th October and 2nd November 1958.

HRH the Duke of Edinburgh visited AEC's Southall Works on 26th November 1957. After touring the factory, the Duke travelled to the factory of Park Royal Vehicles on RM 2.

The third RM was one of the two Leyland engined prototypes. The first variations on the RM code were decided in March 1957 when RM 3 became RML 3 and RM 4 became CRL 4. Neither bus carried its original classification before delivery and RML 3 lost its Leyland suffix in 1962. It was also decided that AEC engined Routemaster coaches would be classified CR. Before delivery this changed to RMC and CRL 4 was reclassified likewise. RML 3 was delivered to London Transport on 1st July 1957 and entered service from Willesden garage on 22nd January 1958.

All four prototypes had different interior colour schemes for the window areas: a deep red on RM 1, light grey on RM 2 (in response to comments that RM 1 felt a little dark inside), mid-grey (officially known as Chinese green) on RML 3 and green on CRL 4. The colour scheme on RML 3 was used on the production RMs. The ceiling colour on the first three prototypes was yellow and on CRL 4 it was cream. The original seating layout on CRL 4 provided seats for 57 passengers, giving increased legroom compared with the bus versions. The capacity was further reduced before the coach entered service by rearranging the seating over the rear wheel arches, where the longitudinal seats were considered undesirable for the longer distance journeys made by Green Line passengers (Green Line RFs had just one single inward facing seat over the front offside wheel). The longitudinal seats were taken out and replaced by armchair style seats set at an angle of about 45 degrees. Longitudinal seating for five was therefore replaced by three individual seats, one on the offside and two on the nearside. This refinement was not carried through to the main batch of RMCs in 1962, which had CRL 4's original seating layout and CRL 4 also reverted to this. The coach had tungsten lighting like the other prototypes. In 1959, Durrant suggested that future Green Line coach Routemasters be fitted with fluorescent lighting, and this suggestion was adopted.

These two views show CRL 4 all round. Its ECW body was completed to a London Transport specification that was similar externally to RML 3, but with platform door added. Note the unique positioning of the offside route number.

London Transport had hoped that Routemaster production would be in full swing from the spring or summer of 1958. The drawings were completed at Chiswick in April. All was not well, however, at Park Royal, where the men submitted claims for substantial improvements in piecework payments just as preparations for RM production were due to start. Only one new RM was ready in 1958, RM 8 being completed before the production line was ready so that it could be displayed on the Park Royal Vehicles stand at that year's Commercial Motor Show. AEC was more advanced, but the new design of gearbox was not ready to go into production, and nor were the wheels. The latter problem resulted in authority being given in June 1958 for AEC to fit the first production RMs with RT-type wheels temporarily. This measure, in the event, proved unnecessary.

Ken Glazier, who worked at 55 Broadway at the time, writes: The engineers had been anxious to get some small scale operational experience with the production model before it was committed to full time service. At the beginning of 1957, when deliveries were still expected to start in the spring of 1958, it was decided to convert route 698 at Bexleyheath ahead of the first stage, so that about twenty buses could be tried in sustained service conditions. Had this happened, Bexleyheath would have run RMs alongside trolleybuses for a few months in 1958 and this appears to have led to second thoughts. By April 1957 the idea was being explored of having a complete changeover at Carshalton, by converting route 654, which required 27 vehicles. Although this solution was preferred by the operators, the engineers did not regard the 654 as being an arduous enough test-bed and suggested that the 611 at Highgate might be more suitable. This would have meant an even longer period of dual operation than might have been envisaged at Bexleyheath and was not acceptable to the operating department. This conflict of interest proved insurmountable and by the time the matter was discussed again in August, it had been decided to operate small quantities of RMs on a number of existing bus routes.

Along with 15 Green Line RFs, CRL 4 received a lighter green livery in 1960. Durrant and Fernyhough were in favour of making this the standard Green Line colour to increase the distinction between Country buses and Green Line coaches, but no further vehicles were done.

66

Park Royal achieved one RM per annum in 1958 and RM 8, seen here being assembled, was it. The RM drawings were completed at Chiswick in April and full production had been due to start in the summer, but labour troubles seriously delayed the setting up of a production line. Park Royal were keen to have a vehicle for display at the 1958 Commercial Motor Show and so this one vehicle was built in advance of full production commencing. In effect it was a prototype for the main batch and spent most of its life out of service and in use for experimental purposes. The exterior panels have been stove enamelled before fitting to the bus, a method of painting that was not carried through to the production run owing to difficulties in preventing scratches and chips.

After completion, RM 8 took part in a number of exercises designed to establish the ease of replacing parts of the bodywork. Here the rear lower deck wall is removed, an operation that first required removal of the lower half of the staircase.

Ready for display at the 1958 Commercial Motor Show, RM 8 had years of use as a Chiswick test bed ahead of it before finally entering passenger service in 1976.

One of the two 'slave chassis' at work. Twenty years earlier, before completion of RT 1, its chassis had been tested beneath the body of an old double-deck TD, which ran in passenger service for a short time numbered ST 1140. For the chassisless RM, using an old bus body to test the units was not an option. The vehicle is seen at Ludgate Circus. Tarpaulins protected the sand bags from rain so that the weight of sand remained unaffected by water.

To test the mechanical components of the Routemaster prior to completed buses being available, London Transport took the unusual step of building two lorry type bodies and mounting these on two sets of sub-frames. Three sets of running units were planned to run as 'slave chassis' (as they were officially called), numbered 001–003, but only 002 and 003 were completed. No.002 ran on route 11 from late summer 1958, soon after joined by 003 working on route 46 (Alperton to Waterloo via Notting Hill Gate).

Both vehicles were intended to be driven following normal service buses to simulate operating conditions as closely as possible. It was the expectation that 001–003 would in due course be employed in RMs 5–7, but in the event the three sets of units were not used in buses until 1960. The two slave chassis subsequently moved to routes 22 and 76 until the entry into service of the first production Routemasters on ordinary bus routes in 1959 made them redundant. The exercise had been of limited value because not all drivers stuck to following a service bus, but instead took the easier option of driving along the route on their own, stopping only when necessary.

The strange looking vehicles, which no doubt aroused the curiosity of the more observant passers by, were fitted with a timber-built driving cab using standard RT cab door and windscreen. The interior of the cab matched the layout of the RM. Alongside was an observation cabin and behind was a platform for carrying sand bags to match the weight of a bus carrying 32 passengers, though sufficient space was provided to match the weight of a fully laden RM. To distribute the weight correctly between the front and rear axles, some of the sand ballast was placed on the roof of the cabin and cab structure.

A surviving report of a test run on route 46 on 25th November 1958 records that the general performance was found to be satisfactory, the only adverse comments being of some throttle vibration against the cab floor plate in certain conditions and that one of the dynamo drive belts had broken.

When the first stage of the trolleybus conversion went ahead, in March 1959, there were still no RMs being delivered from Park Royal. The first were delivered to London Transport in May. Surplus RTs and RTLs were used for the first three conversions and, during this period, London Transport became increasingly concerned about the situation at Park Royal. On 20th May 1959, Durrant reported that the labour difficulties at Park Royal had largely been overcome and that piecework rates had been agreed with the exception of "one or two shops". In fact there were two – the stove enamelling shop and the seat trimming shop. A revised delivery programme was agreed.

Durrant had to further report on 22nd June that Park Royal had failed to meet the revised delivery programme in that, by 19th June, there was a shortfall of 12 in the 52 vehicles that had been due for delivery to AEC by that date. J W Shirley, Director and General Manager at Park Royal, defended the company, pointing out unforeseen problems with weatherproofing of the buses and the adhesive used for the floorcovering. Durrant responded by pointing out that both problems pre-dated the May agreement and that failure of Park Royal to keep to the rate of delivery promised "shook confidence in the ability of PRV to adhere to their undertakings".

Worse, because the problems with the Routemaster bodies had delayed work on buses for other customers, RM production had to be virtually suspended in the second half of June and the early part of July to release men to concentrate on orders for operators outside London. Shirley was now promising 17 RMs in July, 24 in August and 36 each in September and October. These figures would in fact have given more than enough buses for stage four of the trolleybus conversion, but London Transport wanted a large reserve. Shirley wanted to make a special payment to the men to complete 200 buses at the rate of ten per week, with London Transport footing the bill. Durrant did not feel inclined to recommend this, suggesting that it would be preferable to extend the lives of the trolleybuses if necessary.

On 11th September, two months before about 75 RMs would be needed for trolleybus replacement at Poplar and West Ham, Shirley was summoned to a meeting at Chiswick to report on the latest position. He read a prepared statement. There were still two major shops pressing for improvements in pay rates, one of which had already staged a half-day unofficial strike that week (a complete ban on overtime working had been imposed by the men). A third department, that had agreed new rates a few months earlier, was now disputing the agreement. "Work is continuing meantime," reported Shirley, "but in none of the three departments wherein piecework prices are the subject of dispute is a proper piecework effort being made, and indeed the tempo is quite unsatisfactory". The prepared statement acknowledged that Park Royal had been fighting a losing battle on piecework prices for nearly two years, and changing conditions in industry made it difficult to make progress. The only way in which he would be prepared to guarantee any delivery programme would be on the basis of London Transport being prepared to accept the cost of the demands being made by the men. His company's competitive quote had clearly left him little room for manoeuvre.

London Transport may now have been having some regrets about having put all of its eggs in the Park Royal basket. There is little doubt that the men at the factory felt they were in a strong bargaining position. Following the reading of Shirley's prepared statement at Chiswick, the Executive sought legal advice about its contract with the company and in particular whether the situation gave London Transport grounds for termination of the contract. After checking the wording, the lawyers informed the Executive that this was not an option. London Transport did have the right to take over the materials, jigs, tools and fixtures produced for the RM body to pass to another builder in the event of interruption of supply, but setting up elsewhere would take time. In addition it was felt likely that the trades unions would cause the same problems at any factory in which building the Routemaster might be contemplated, so this was not a real option.

The front and rear sub-frames of the Routemaster were delivered from AEC's works at Southall by lorry to Park Royal with the mechanical units in place, save for the gearbox which was supplied separately to be attached directly under the body shell. The vehicle thus 'came to life', first able to move under it own power, at Park Royal. RM 12 leaves Park Royal Vehicles in May 1959 for a final check at AEC before delivery to London Transport.

It is not known whether London Transport seriously intended to take the contract away from Park Royal or whether it just wanted to make the threat in the hope it would bring an end to the staff unrest. In a report on the situation in September 1959, Durrant wrote "clearly the men are trying to force the issue on piecework earnings by delaying tactics, believing that, in jeopardising the trolleybus conversion, they will force the Executive to foot the bill for the extra cost involved. PRV know this to be so and we have heard it from independent sources on their shop floor".

Thoughts turned to the possibility of delaying the trolleybus conversion from stage five onwards for up to a year if necessary. After seeking the views of all those in charge of running and maintaining the trolleybus system, this became option number one in the event of continuing delays in RM production. No such delay to the conversion programme proved necessary, however, as not long after the 11th September meeting at Chiswick, a settlement was reached which enabled Shirley's promise of 36 RMs a month to be kept. Between September 1959 and April 1960 the monthly total of RM deliveries to London Transport averaged 35, or 36 if allowance is made for the Christmas shutdown. This was sufficient for London Transport's needs and there were no further interruptions in delivery on account of labour disputes.

Lightweight but Lasting

Between RM 1 as originally built and RM 8, half a ton was added to the weight of the Routemaster through improvements to the design. It was still one of the lightest double deckers of its time, writes Alan Townsin in this survey.

Possibly the greatest hidden virtue of the Routemaster is its modest weight, all the more remarkable when judged today at the end of a remarkably long operational career with none of the survivors less than 37 years old, mostly having been in use continuously over that time, with no more than short breaks for overhauls etc. When the specification was planned in 1951, an operational life of 15 years was widely regarded as quite a lengthy target and a life of 18 years was planned for the RM. Speaking at an internal LT meeting in August 1959, Durrant expressed his view that each vehicle could achieve an economical life of 25 years, a longevity unheard of at the time.

Light construction was an avowed aim of London Transport's engineers from the outset, aware as they were that the amount of fuel consumed by a city bus requiring to be repeatedly accelerated from rest is directly influenced by its weight. Yet there is nothing flimsy about the construction or skimped in terms of finish.

The unladen weight of the standard post-war RT type 56-seat bus as introduced in 1947 was 7 tons 10 cwt (7620kg); it was still in large-scale production when the initial specification for the Routemaster was set down on paper in 1951. This was a fairly typical weight for a two axle double decker of 26ft length and 7ft 6in width built in the period up to 1950 when these dimensions were the maximum for general operation, although from 1946 it had been permissible to operate 8ft wide buses on specified routes approved by the Traffic Commissioners. Then general approval for operation of two-axle double deckers of up to 27ft length and 8ft width came into effect from June 1950, although the RT continued in production with unchanged dimensions until output ceased in 1954.

When the Routemaster prototype was completed in time for the Commercial Motor Show of September 1954, its unladen weight proved to be 6 tons 14 cwt 2 qr (6833kg) – in other words, its unladen weight was equivalent to only 90% of that of the RT despite being built to the new dimensions and having seats for 64 passengers.

This figure was reminiscent of double decker weights of the period shortly before the 1939-45 war – a typical London Transport STL 56-seater weighed 6 tons 12 cwt. At that time the gross weight, including passengers and crew, fuel etc, was limited to 10½ tons, a very tight restriction which effectively limited a 56-seater to about 6¾ tons unladen. This made it difficult to make the body structure durable on the basis of standard timber-framed constructional methods of that time, although buses were then rarely expected to last much beyond 10 years and, in London, the practice was for them to receive quite frequent body overhauls, carried out to high standards. The STL buses, retained far longer than planned when built due to the effects of the war, had required major body rebuilds in their later years.

The first published reference to the possibility of an RM running in unpainted condition appeared in the March 1957 issue of the London Transport Magazine, but it was to be nearly four years before one was left unpainted for inspection. London Transport had placed its first unpainted aluminium Underground train in service in January 1953 and in 1954 Liverpool Corporation had been the first British bus company to put an unpainted aluminium bus into service, a measure aimed at reducing painting costs rather than saving weight. In the case of the RM the weight saving was just 1 cwt, giving a small – virtually negligible – improvement in fuel economy. Unpainted RM 664 was inspected at the Park Royal factory by members of the Executive on 8th February 1961. It was to be another six months before it was officially taken into stock, during which there was further consideration of the idea. Durrant was not enthusiastic, pointing out in a report dated 7th April 1961 that the cost savings of running buses in unpainted condition were quite small and that the complications of keeping

unpainted aluminium panels in presentable condition could well outweigh any savings in painting costs. Road vehicles were frequently grazed or more badly damaged in contact with other vehicles and, as aluminium changed in colour with use, replacing panels would be more difficult. Weight saving had always been a secondary consideration to savings in painting costs, but this was the only area where a cost saving could be guaranteed. This saving was, however, negligible and estimated by Durrant at £3 per bus per year. He concluded his report by saying that there was no real financial saving to be obtained by operating buses in unpainted condition, partly because of the very economical painting process in use at Aldenham. Nevertheless, RM 664 entered service unpainted in July 1961 and ran for four years in this condition. Public Relations Office files indicate that public comments were fairly equally balanced between praise and criticism, but the bus weathered less well than the traditionally painted RMs and it was painted red in 1965.

When the gross weight limit was raised, at first because of wartime shortages of aluminium and later to allow for larger dimensions, it gave greater freedom of action. Manufacturers and operators generally accepted increased weight in a search for greater durability – use of cast iron instead of aluminium alloy for engine castings etc had been found to produce units which could run longer between overhauls and sturdier bodywork, often metal-framed, usually lasted longer too. It was by no means uncommon for 27ft x 8ft double deckers being built for other fleets to weigh over 8 tons by the early 1950s.

By 1951 the gross weight limit set by legislation was 12 tons but London Transport decided to aim for 11½ tons, despite the increased seating capacity. Careful design led to further lightening and the prototype as completed was actually 3 cwt (152kg) less than the figure estimated in advance.

Rising costs were just beginning to awaken the industry's awareness of the need for a tighter attitude to weight, other ventures in that vein in 1952 including the Leyland Tiger Cub single decker and the MCW Orion double-deck body, though these involved some sacrifice of passenger refinement, with smaller and 'fussier' fast-revving engines and often skimping on standards of interior finish and trim. The London Transport team resolutely avoided such an approach and indeed were seeking improved standards, for example in better ride comfort from independent front suspension and coil springs all round.

The first example of a production Routemaster to be completed was RM 8, exhibited at the 1958 Commercial Motor Show, this being 27ft 6½in long and its unladen weight quoted as 7 tons 5 cwt (736kg), these figures also applying to subsequent standard RM buses. The half-ton increase in weight compared with RM 1 in original condition resulted mostly from the improved specification – interior heating, power-assisted steering, front-mounted radiator and larger destination blind boxes. Although this figure represented an increase of just under 8% on that of the prototype as built four years earlier, the vehicle was the lightest double decker at the Show. Some other operators were achieving similar weights but again only with more austere specifications.

On the RML, the unladen weight was increased by 10 cwt, becoming 7 tons 15 cwt (7872kg) and, in terms of weight per seated passenger, gave an even better figure (241lb/passenger) than the standard RM. The heaviest Routemasters with the exception of FRM 1 were the 30ft long Green Line coach RCLs, which weighed in at 8 tons (8128kg). Even the 31ft 3ins long FRM, with more complex specification, had the creditable weight of 8 tons 10 cwt (8636kg), about one ton less than the 30ft 6ins long Daimler Fleetlines that were ordered for RT and Routemaster replacement. In the event, of course, the Routemaster outlived these.

Towards a Bigger Bus

The increase in maximum permitted length of two-axle double deckers from 27ft to 30ft in July 1956 and the completion of mechanisation of ticket issue on London buses in 1958 paved the way for more seats.

The London General Omnibus Company ran a few 70 and 72 seater buses in the late 1920s when it had a small batch of 29ft 8¼in London Six three-axle double deckers of varying seating capacity. All had been downseated to 56 by the end of 1934 because of the difficulties presented to the conductor in collecting all the fares. As mentioned earlier in the book, proposals for 70-seater buses were made again in 1939 and 1949. In September 1958 comparative checks were made of uncollected fares on the RT and the 70-seater trolleybus. These gave figures of 1.7% uncollected fares on RTs and 2.9% on the trolleybuses. These figures were better than those of six years earlier, before the introduction of the Gibson ticket machine, but the trolleybuses did not run along the busiest central London streets where the uncollected fares could be expected to be greater. Nevertheless, in January 1960 Durrant is recorded as saying that he was investigating the enlargement of the Routemaster to a 70-seater. Two months later, Central Bus Operating Manager John Burnell stated that it remained his view that in the conditions of central London, the size of bus ought not to be increased above 64 seats.

Notwithstanding the Operating Manager's view, in April 1960 the Executive asked Burnell and Durrant to examine whether the street conditions of central London were suitable for a bus of 30ft length. To help answer this question, an AEC Bridgemaster was driven along the complete lengths of routes 3, 11, 22 and 30 and was also used to negotiate selected junctions on other routes, some of which presented "real difficulty", they reported. Two turns on route 25 were mentioned in their joint report: the one from Oxford Street into New Bond Street and the one from Piccadilly into Old Bond Street. Subject to special care being taken by the drivers of the 30ft long buses, it was estimated that up to 1,000 buses of the greater length could be made use of in the Central Bus area subject to individual route approval by the licensing authorities.

By the early part of 1961 a decision had been taken to order a small trial batch of 30ft long Routemasters, with 72 seats. The extra seating accommodation was in the form of an extra row of two pairs of seats on each deck. The addition of a half-length bay of 2ft 4ins in the centre of the bus gave a total length of 29ft 10½ins. Longitudinal stiffeners in the body structure were specified to provide additional strength. This method of increasing the length meant that almost all other parts remained common to the existing vehicle, of obvious value in terms of manufacture and spares. Minor changes were the longer propeller shaft and slightly larger tyres.

Of more relevance to the manoeuvrability than the length of the bus was the wheelbase. The Bridgemaster that had been used to survey a number of routes had a wheelbase of 18ft 10ins, but the RML's wheelbase was 19ft 2ins. The method of producing RMLs, about which there is more in the Building the Bodies chapter, meant that there was no scope for reducing the wheelbase. However, as with the caution over the RTWs when they were new, the fears that drivers would have difficulty proved unfounded.

AEC's Bridgemaster used a number of ideas from the Routemaster design and AEC paid London Transport a small royalty on each bus sold. Although London Transport was already operating 30ft long vehicles through central London in the form of RF Green Line coaches, the layout of these gave a wheelbase of 16ft 4ins. To survey some central London routes with a 30ft long double decker, London Transport used a Bridgemaster, with a wheelbase 2ft 6ins longer.

RMF 1254 was a unique (for London) variation of the RML, delivered in 1962. This had seats for 38 passengers upstairs and 31 down, giving a total capacity three smaller than that of the RML.

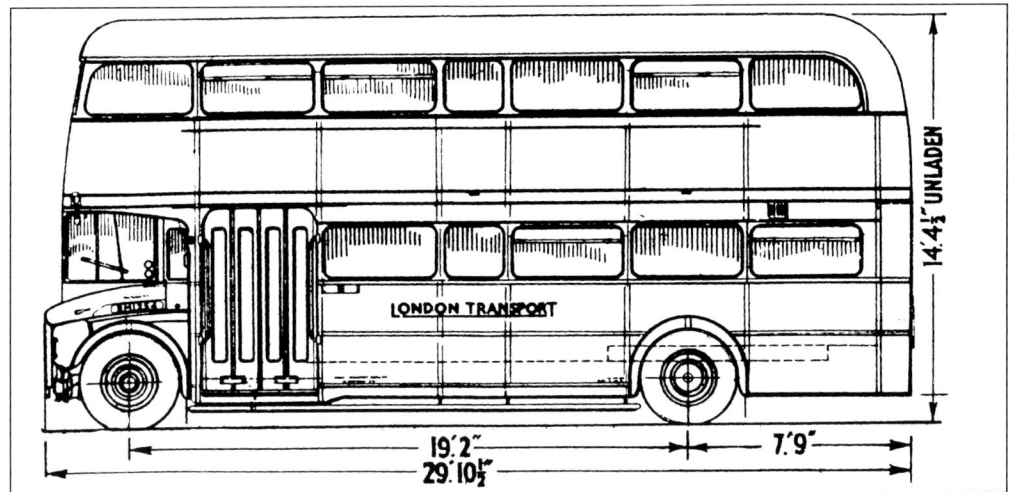

After running 19 of the 24 RMLs on a former trolleybus route, it was another four years before any more arrived, but in 1962 a front entrance version of the RML was designed and built. Then, in 1965, a batch of 50 Leyland Atlanteans arrived for comparison in service with RMLs. Platform doors for double-deck buses had been subjected to boarding and alighting time trials (probably using CRL 4) at Chiswick Works in 1958, following which the Executive decided that the number and amount of injury claims from passengers falling off the platform was insufficient to justify the delay at stops and extra cost of adding doors to the specification. Doors on front entrance buses were another matter. Apart from their function of cutting out unnecessary draughts, there was added justification from the fact that they could be controlled by the driver, freeing the conductor to collect the fares. In this respect the Atlantean was preferable in layout to the RMF. From 1965 all new double deckers were to be of the 30ft length until even longer vehicles were permitted by revised regulations.

Early Problems

When Routemasters first entered service in large numbers in replacement of trolleybuses, their service running was far from trouble-free. Indeed over the life of the design, around 2,000 modifications had to be made to it despite the pre-production trials. Ken Blacker writes about these early years of problem running.

The Routemaster is a phenomenon, the like of which will probably never be repeated. This chapter looks back on the early days of its operation and, in doing so, turns the clock back a full forty years and more. It is nothing short of incredible that a bus built in the 1950s and 1960s should still have been in service in the first years of the 21st century. Admittedly most were much modified, but still the basic structure remained the same, serving as a testimony to all those who designed and then maintained the vehicles through their long and arduous careers. The sheer longevity of the Routemaster is put into its true perspective when you consider that those of us within the bus industry who were still young when the RM first went into quantity production have since worked through the whole of our long careers, witnessing vast changes in the process, and have now reached the point where, if alive at all, are well into retirement. All the while, the Routemaster has been a focal point on the London scene.

The Routemaster is now firmly entrenched as part of bus folklore and deservedly so, but much less well remembered is the fact that it enjoyed anything but a good reputation in its early days. It started out, in fact, as an engineer's nightmare, and its impact on service reliability was at first disastrous.

To start with, production had got under way late because of industrial problems, leaving inadequate time for test running before the first full-scale operation was implemented with stage 4 of the trolleybus conversion programme on 11th November 1959. Prior to this, between 6th June and 1st November 1959, 45 RMs were licensed for passenger service at six garages, though because some had already been delicensed before others came on the road, the number theoretically available for service never exceeded 40. During this period of experimental running, with never more than eight RMs allocated to any of the trial garages at any one time, problems would have been manageable. The records that have survived indicate problems with cracks appearing in part of the B frames, minor electrical failures, noisy brakes and some leakage of brake fluid. What stands out clearly is the fact that trial running seems to have left no-one with any inkling as to the disaster that was to occur from 11th November onwards.

Stage 4 was concentrated solely on the three trolleybus services (567, 569 and 665) serving the heart of the East End via the Commercial Road with various offshoots at each end. These were frequent and extremely well patronised, particularly at peak periods, and their demise saw the end of trolleybuses at Poplar depot and the first incursion (out of three) of motorbuses into West Ham. Poplar's initial scheduled RM requirement of 59 was augmented by four additional vehicles serving as engineering spares, whilst West Ham received one spare to augment its scheduled working commitment of 14.

The fairly smooth operation of RMs on RT family routes between June and the beginning of November 1959 gave no clue to the massive problems that would occur when larger numbers were used to replace trolleybuses.

In hindsight the allocation of such a low percentage of spares, when the vehicles concerned were of a completely new, innovative and virtually untried type, was risky. It was based on established RT practice, but – as the engineers soon found out to their cost – the early Routemaster was a very different essay in reliability from the RT.

Prior to the conversion all depot engineering staff had to be trained on diesel engined vehicles, and on the intricacies of the RM in particular. Everybody was given two weeks thorough instruction, which also intended to serve as an indoctrination into the superiority of the diesel bus over the vehicles that they had been used to. Despite this, difficulties in attitude arose, some of which had been simmering for up to twelve months due to the disruption of working conditions while rebuilding took place to accommodate the new vehicles, compounded by the morale-sapping knowledge that the trolleybus fleet, which had been their livelihood for so long, was on its way out. Very many remained unconvinced that the new vehicles offered any improvement on the old. It was against this background that the first trolleybus replacement Routemaster, RM 82, set out on its historic journey from Poplar garage for Charing Cross shortly before midnight on 10th/11th November.

RM 62 was one of the Routemasters allocated to Poplar for stage four of the trolleybus conversion. It displays blinds for a new route replacing a trolleybus night service, which was extended to Charing Cross.

Right Route 23 was an example of an existing bus service that was strengthened to participate in trolleybus replacement. For this it received an allocation of RMs from Poplar. New into service, RM 84 is seen at Becontree Heath.

Wednesday 11th November 1959 turned out to be the ultimate busman's nightmare. In a single day, engineers at Poplar and West Ham took more than one hundred road calls from drivers in trouble. Comparing this against perhaps three or four calls a day received under the old trolleybus regime, it is easy to see that they quickly became completely overwhelmed. Some calls were made simply because drivers were unfamiliar with the new vehicles and could be dealt with by a few words of advice, but the clear majority related to specific defects each of which needed to be put right. The most memorable fault of the day was of gearbox air systems failing to 'cut in', but numerous other problems also surfaced with which the engineering staff were to become only too familiar over the coming months. The now-superseded trolleybuses may have suffered their ups and downs, and could be particularly frustrating at times of power failure when mass delays occurred, but overall it was recognised that they had provided a satisfactory and reliable service which, in their early days, Routemasters were simply unable to replicate.

New route 5, on which RM 32 is seen at Bloomsbury, had the highest allocation of RMs in stage four and would have been affected by the many problems suffered by the early RMs. Nevertheless, the Public Relations Officer was able to report to the Executive that the new services had been received with few complaints to him.

The weeks passed by, and although the worst of the initial chaos abated, the overall situation remained dire. A whole host of problems surfaced on the RMs, some due to design defects and others due to faulty manufacture. To the credit of the engineering staff, relatively few problems occurred due to poor maintenance even though, through lack of experience, they were often unable to diagnose and deal with faults as quickly as those brought up with motorbuses might have done. The new vehicles were very complex, and this was particularly felt by the electricians who, though highly competent in dealing with trolleybus electrical systems, were unaccustomed to the sheer complexity of the RM's electrics. The overall problem was further compounded by an increase in the accident rate, perhaps due to drivers' unfamiliarity with the new vehicles, and whereas the garages found that replacement mechanical parts were relatively easy to procure, this was not the case in the early days with coach material needed to repair body damage.

The electrical system was responsible for a high percentage of Routemaster failures, notably the 'Arens' master control equipment. Windscreen wiper defects were also especially prevalent, and high on the problem agenda were gear selector switches, microswitches, starter switches, bell and hooter wiring, and batteries. On the mechanical side shock absorbers and rubbers needed frequent changing, gearbox seals were grossly inadequate, radiator fans and water pumps were often defective, and the exhaust system was a source of continuous trouble. The gearboxes, which for the most part gave an unacceptably jerky ride, suffered excessive slipping and sticking, with top speeds particularly prone to becoming defective. As was to be expected the engines performed well enough although many problems were recorded on the auxiliaries including defective injectors and fuel pumps, along with numerous spring failures on the throttle mechanism, whilst serious brake troubles (often related to bursting or otherwise unsatisfactory hydraulic pipes) were a frequent source of drivers' reports. On the bodywork, roller blind equipment became unworkable far too often and the heaters on almost every vehicle proved unreliable. Drivers' seats began to fracture and become unsafe from an early stage, whilst the material filling the seat squabs soon began to collapse, giving the passenger a feeling that he or she had 'grounded' when sitting down.

From the very start, modification programmes were instituted with the aim of trying to overcome permanently each ongoing problem as it arose, and as vehicle deliveries progressed upon which modifications had already been incorporated, so the overall performance level improved. However back in the winter of 1959/1960 that happy situation had still to be reached. Some modifications were carried out in the two garages, but because staff were so preoccupied with the day-to-day work of keeping the buses running, other modifications had to be applied elsewhere. After running for less than a month, twelve of Poplar's RMs were delicensed on 1st December to check for steering column fractures, followed by a further ten on 1st January 1960. They were replaced by vehicles (some new and others that had run experimentally in the June to November period) already checked out and modified in a number of ways. This gave the overworked staff at Poplar a little breathing space, but over at West Ham stage 5 of the conversion programme was due to be implemented on 3rd February 1960 followed by stage 6 on 27th April, and at this much larger premises the effects of the ongoing problems simply multiplied. Another garage, Walthamstow, was also involved in both of these conversions and the same tale of woe applied there too.

The sheer scale of the Routemasters' initial tribulations inevitably reflected negatively on those who had to work with them. Whatever their capacity, whether it was engineering, driving/conducting, or as a supervisor attempting to produce a semblance of good service, the uncertainty was demoralising. Morale as a whole, amongst former trolleybus men, was not too good anyway. Many were resentful that their coveted working practices had been superseded by the busmen's agreements, especially since the latter were generally more restrictive and much less flexible than they had been used to. Whether they

RM 335 was one of the buses allocated to Shepherd's Bush garage to replace trolleybuses from Hammersmith depot. During the summer of 1959, complaints had been received from passengers about the non-opening front windows on the early RMs, leading to openers being fitted on new deliveries from February 1960.

liked it or not, all trolleybus employees had been obliged to accept the revised working agreements upon payment of a lump sum, since this was what their unions had negotiated with London Transport's management. At the time, the unions operated a 'closed shop' policy (with London Transport's blessing, it must be said), giving them virtual control of all supervisory and manual staff. It was in line with their current thinking to encourage restrictive working practices as much as possible in order to tighten their negotiating grip, but this inevitably resulted in former trolleybus staff becoming scornful of a management which condoned the setting up of demarcation lines where they had not existed before. The resultant decline in efficiency, leading to increased costs and poorer performance, were there for all to see.

It was 'on the road' that the restrictive practices hit hardest. The most difficult one for trolleybus men to swallow was the rule that, whatever the circumstances, a bus must not be diverted for operational reasons from the route to which it was allocated. This meant that gaps to one particular destination, however caused, could no longer be plugged by switching resources in the time honoured way, thereby failing to make the best use of available buses and crews. This, and various other restrictive arrangements, were hangovers from pre-war bus days and their potential impact had been hardly noticed at times when every duty was always covered and buses seldom broke down. However with the arrival of the Routemasters, supervisors found themselves severely hamstrung in responding to the serious gaps or, conversely, the unacceptable bunching that could occur so unpredictably. Their hands were tied, too, by another restriction preventing them from anticipating problems which they knew from experience were likely to arise, such as severe traffic congestion at known blackspots like Canning Town, which meant that they were no longer able to take the necessary corrective action in advance. In the end the main sufferers were, of course, the passengers, for whom the standard of service plummeted when the Routemaster era arrived.

Behind the scenes everything possible was being done to find the cause of each new problem on the Routemaster as it arose and to try to devise a remedy. A modification programme was set in hand, the full extent of which can be gauged by the fact that, between November 1959 and October 1961, no fewer than 55 'advice notes' were issued from Chiswick relating to mechanical alterations, plus a further 24 applying to electrical items and 38 to bodywork, most of which needed to be carried out on every RM in the fleet at the time of issue. On top of all this, many of the early RMs were the subject of experiments each of which had to be monitored and documented, and the results sent back to Chiswick. The almost unbelievable scale of this can be illustrated by the fact that, in November 1961, no fewer than 25 separate experiments were being carried out on vehicles at West Ham garage alone, quite apart from those at other locations. Some of these were multiple experiments involving more than one vehicle; in fact a total of 229 experimental items were fitted to no fewer than 115 RMs in the West Ham fleet. Some were large scale experiments, such as the use of alkaline instead of lead acid batteries; others covered a wide sphere ranging from experiments on Clayton Dewandre and Westinghouse air compressors, various types of shock absorbers, engine stop controls, radiator fans, saloon water pipes, windscreen wipers and a miscellany of other things besides. As if these were not enough for the garage staff to worry about, there were also various deviations from standard specified at the manufacturing stage that were not, strictly speaking, part of the ongoing experimental programme but nevertheless added complications to the maintenance schedule. Examples of this were the DC electrical system with dynamo drive (instead of the usual AC system with alternator) on RMs 5-21, 341, 398 and 459 and the four different types of rear-end air suspension (in place of coil springs) on RMs 75 and 87-135.

In April 1960 the District Engineer whose 'patch' included West Ham and Poplar retired through ill health and was replaced by Charles Greystock who later achieved high office within the organisation. He did much to systematically tackle the serious problems with which he was confronted and to develop the good team spirit necessary for success. This alone presented quite a formidable task. Quite apart from the general low morale inherent in an overworked staff, West Ham had 'inherited' the former busmen from Forest Gate garage when it closed on 27th April 1960, and the two groups of staff simply would not mix. Even in the canteen at mealtimes they chose habitually to sit separately. This was not, in fact, a condition unique to West Ham; it occurred wherever former trolleybus and bus employees were brought together as in the mergers of Bow and Clay Hall, or of Wood Green and West Green, and it was indicative of the very different attitudes prevailing within the two traditions.

RM 301 has broken down in service from West Ham garage and a mechanic has been called out to see if it can be fixed on the road. He can just be made out under the bus.

It is thanks to records which Charles Greystock has kindly supplied that we are able to look back more than forty years to detail the true magnitude of the task as it applied to one garage, West Ham. They are statistics that would make any bus engineer's hair rise in astonishment. Today all would baulk at the sheer cost and manpower implications of tackling such a magnitude of work; their first thought would be to return the offending vehicles to the manufacturer under warranty as being grossly unsatisfactory. Between May 1960 and August 1961, on an RM fleet averaging 142 buses, the changes of equipment listed below were carried out. The list is by no means exhaustive but merely documents the major tasks that were tackled; very many others were recorded too.

Mechanical: 518 brake shoe liners; 425 gearbox seals; 416 front shock absorber rubbers; 393 top speed shims; 302 handbrake trigger rod stops; 249 jacking pads; 247 alternator belts; 195 exhaust tail pipe straps and brackets; 186 radiator fans; 144 compressor belts; 138 water pumps; 126 rear shock absorbers; 101 front shock absorbers; 90 gearbox adjuster springs; 46 radiators; 29 Lockheed brake cylinders, etc.

Electrical: 121 wiper arms and blades; 119 Arens controls; 114 flashing indicator bulbs; 82 gear switches; 78 Simms rectifiers; 39 windscreen wiper units; 33 looms and loops of all types; 30 starters, etc.

Bodywork: 149 cab 'Pyrene' brackets; 143 driver's seat frames; 143 platform sill edges; 140 cab door top runners; 140 leaking cab doors; 140 buses with seat squabs loose in the top channel; 140 'Duvina' (a type of rexine) coverings on rear destination box doors worn; 140 burgundy paintwork faulty on platforms and staircases; 117 fractured screws on stanchion rails; 102 cab door finger pulls; 91 failures of adhesion on floor slatting and tiles; 83 waistrail bolts on seats loose; 82 rear destination box door bracket assemblies; 77 unsatisfactory exterior paintwork; 74 spindle keyway breakages on heater regulators; 68 buses with caving-in of seat squab material; 61 bent platform stanchions under service conditions, etc.

As conversion succeeded conversion, and more and more RMs entered service, the survival techniques acquired in the first traumatic two years stood the engineering department in good stead. Greater reliability was gradually achieved, as indeed it had to be. London Transport was totally committed to the Routemaster and there could be no turning back. In April 1963 a fully comprehensive, year long review of all aspects of the design was undertaken with the aim of clearing all the bugs out of system once and for all. This really marked the turning point from which sprang the much-vaunted high reputation largely associated with the Routemaster in more recent times. Through subsequent experimentation, and trial and error, the means of dealing effectively with A and B frame defects, of achieving smooth transmission, of designing a trustworthy heating system, and of overcoming a host of other problems to attain a good standard of reliability, were gradually learnt.

Building the Bodies

John Aldridge is a transport journalist who made a number of visits to Park Royal when the Routemaster was being built in the early 1960s. Here he writes about what was to be seen at the factory.

Park Royal had, of course, been closely involved with the first two prototype RMs, which were built at Chiswick. But while LT was obliged to buy a major quantity of its chassis or mechanical requirements from AEC there was no similar requirement for bodywork. Building the third prototype by Weymann and the fourth by ECW suggested that the contract for series production was not an absolute certainty, even though ECW's involvement might be regarded as mere gesture by LT to its masters, the British Transport Commission. But ECW's commitment to the Tilling Group, also BTC controlled, meant it would have had to build large extensions to its Lowestoft plant to accommodate any large LT order or divert its work for Scottish Bus Group and Tilling customers elsewhere.

But there was plenty of spare capacity in the bus bodybuilding industry and many – including Park Royal – were also bodying vans and lorries to keep their works and workers occupied. However, only Park Royal and Weymann had experience of jig-building on a large scale as undertaken by them for RT-type bodies. But the higher build rate of those halcyon days had also allowed the costs of jigs and setting up to be spread over a larger number of bodies constructed in a shorter timespan. There was also the fundamental difference between an RT and an RM body in that the former contained considerable timber. So calculating the likely, or hoped for, number of man-hours in an RM structure was extremely difficult, albeit with the likely outcome of a much larger stable workload than could be obtained from any other contract.

Park Royal, like Weymann or MCW, had also had experience of building integral vehicles. MCW had built a large number of very successful trolleybuses for London in the late 1930s and post-war co-operation with Leyland produced the Olympic single decker while the Park Royal-AEC Monocoach was an integral version of the AEC Reliance. But the Monocoach had sufficient underframe strength for the 'chassis' to be able to be driven to Park Royal for completion, whereas the Routemaster had a complete structure on to which necessary parts would be hung. Furthermore a very high degree of accuracy was required and, for example, after assembly at Park Royal the front A frame with engine, front wheels, steering and other components was checked on a steel frame representing the cab for clearances and wheel alignment. Many components came directly to Park Royal so there were storage and fitting times to be calculated for these too.

No doubt there was a feeling of great relief when Park Royal heard it had won the order to build the initial 850 buses. Quite drastic pruning of the estimated costs probably helped: this had certainly worried some in the company's small management team when the bid went in. But once production got under way it was estimated that 1,970 man-hours went into a Routemaster at Park Royal, against 2,400 hours for an RT body. Part of the difference was because of the timber content of the RT body, while another part was because virtually every body component for the RM was jig-built.

The Park Royal factory, beside the Grand Union Canal, with one of the first RMs to come off the production line seen in the company of a 30ft long East Kent Regent V, with even more of an upright front than the RM, and an overseas single decker. East Kent was one of the first companies to take full advantage of the increased legal length.

Until the coming of the Leyland National, Park Royal's Routemaster facilities were the most efficient and relatively automated bus building set-up in the UK. Yet the same plant in the same factory was also building conventional bus bodies (and sometimes even coach bodies) as well as AEC lorry cabs and – for several years – the body shells for high-quality Bristol cars. A commercial contract, the last-mentioned was seen as a means of encouraging apprentices and qualified staff to attain high standards.

From a technical point of view LT's decision to go for an aluminium chassisless structure was way ahead of the thinking of the rest of the industry. Aluminium is considerably lighter than, though not as strong as, steel but the inherent lightness of aluminium means that critical components can be deeper or wider to give both stiffness and strength. LT's experience as head of the London Aircraft Production consortium originally based at Aldenham – Park Royal was another member – was one of the main reasons for its enthusiasm for both aluminium and jig-building, and of course it had already gained much experience with the 175 MCW-bodied trolleybuses in the late 1930s.

But the decision to go for aluminium alloy chassisless construction was nevertheless courageous. A box structure, as in the Routemaster, is inherently strong. There are the underframe, floor, sides and roof, plus front and rear bulkheads and an intermediate floor (the upper deck) to provide added rigidity. The underframe incorporated crossbearers of 'I' shaped high duty alloy, with 'H' section pillars bolted to them with angle brackets. The upper deck pillars were of similar section but lighter. Support for the upper deck floor came from further 'I' shaped bearers, but these were not as deep as the underframe ones. Wheelboxes at the rear and the footstalls were also particularly rigid as they also formed beams for the rear suspension. The front bulkhead was also of particularly robust construction as it formed the main anchorage for attachment of the front A frame carrying the engine. It was designed to spread the load evenly across the bulkhead. An echo of RT body design came with the alloy-framed and alloy-sheeted rear platform floor which was suspended from the upper deck. The framing of the back of the bus below upper deck level was designed to be easily removable in sections, with the staircase split at the fourth tread. At the front, the cab was also cantilevered off the front bulkhead in similar fashion to that of an RT. Lifting and jacking points were built into the structure to simplify removal and replacement of A and B frames – tasks that were normally to be carried out at the Aldenham overhaul works, though after London's country buses were handed to the National Bus Company, London Country found it was possible to remove a B frame in a garage and without special equipment, a job first achieved at its Northfleet garage.

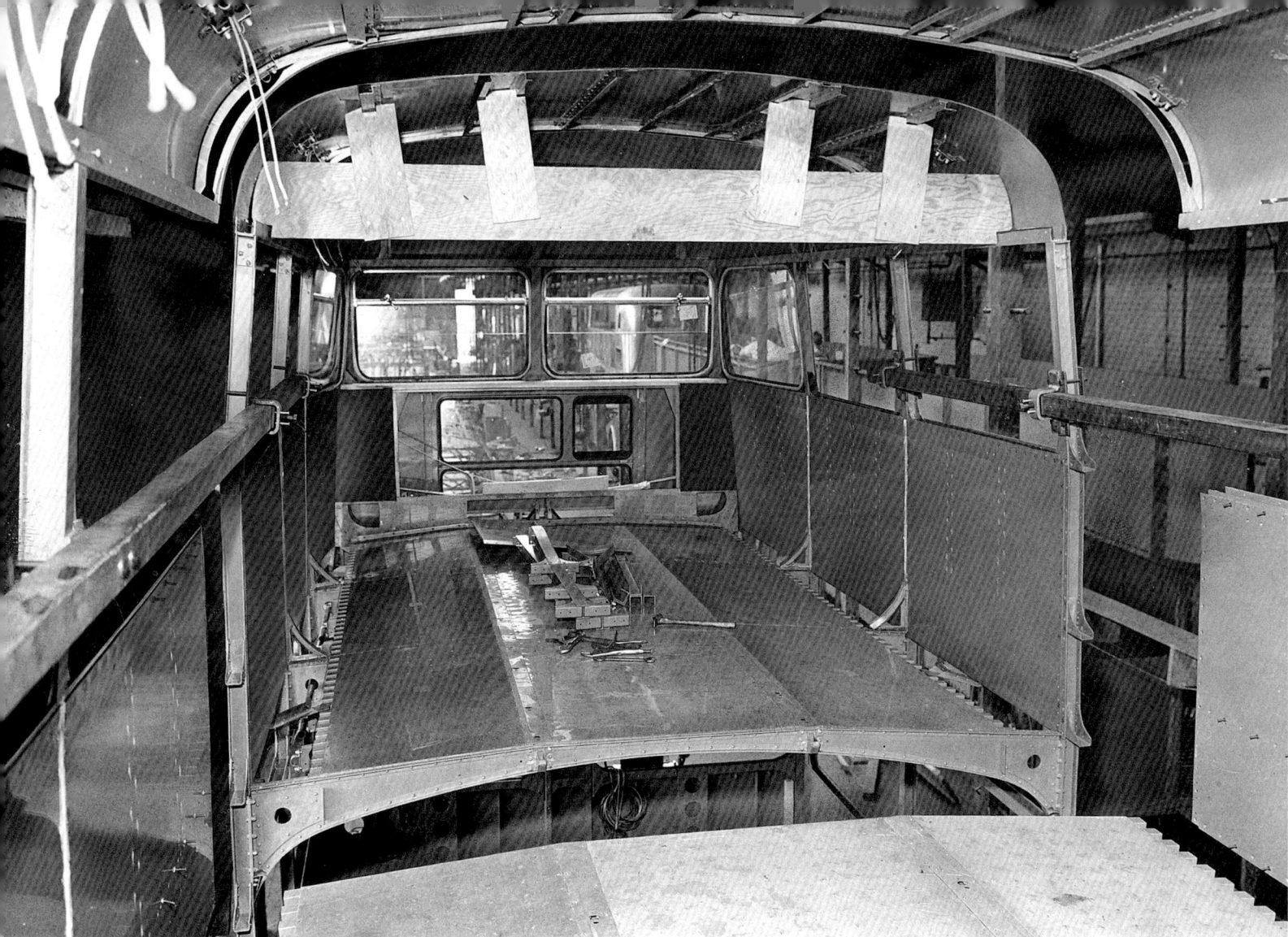

The exhaustive testing certainly produced a durable structure, as evidenced by the number of Routemasters still around. But the design, or rather, its length was soon overtaken by the increase in legal length for double deckers. As recorded earlier, LT at first responded only by moving the radiator on the prototypes to a more sensible and reliable position ahead of the engine, instead of underneath, but eventually a trial batch of a modest 24 72-seaters was built in 1961 within an overall length of 29ft 10⁹⁄₁₆ins.

For Park Royal the main concern was the problem of shoehorning a batch of different buses in among a continuing run of standardised vehicles – delivery was spread over nearly six months, during which over 200 standard RMs were produced. The long vehicles were built on the same production line in the same way as short buses, except that one pillar on each side, together with its attendant roof frame, was bolted into position instead of riveted. When that was completed, the complete vehicle as it stood was moved off the production line to a side shop. By this time, the mechanical components had been installed, the upper deck was fitted (upper decks with roofs were built separately) but the external panelling and lower deck floor were not fitted. By this means the accurately controlled flow system of components, with sub-assemblies built on jigs and fed into the assembly line at the right place and time, were all undisturbed.

Above and Right The trial batch of RMLs was built on the production line with RMs, but with one section bolted. Elaborate precautions were taken, using a steel framework to maintain structural accuracy and integrity before the bolts were removed, the sections jacked apart and a new short centre section added.

In the adjacent body shop the two halves of the body were separated and the additional 2ft 4in wide bay added between them. But considerable care was taken before the two halves were unbolted. A steel framework was bolted on top of the cross-bearers in the front part of the body. It consisted of longitudinal rails, diagonal bracing and a cross-piece. The rails extended into the rear section of the body where they engaged with other rails similarly fastened to the rear body underframe and there was another steel frame in the rear part complete with temporary timber arches to support the intermediate floor and roof. The rear of the front half of the body was supported on two jacks. Only then were the temporary bolts between the two halves removed and the sections separated with a hand-operated screw jack gradually pushing the sections further apart. Then the additional pillars, roof supports and extra cross-bearers were fitted. Stress panels, flooring, roof panels and other items were now added and the temporary supports removed.

Not until May 1965 would more long Routemasters be built, and then the whole production line went over to them, the first 43 all being Green Line coaches. The idea of an extra half bay, as found on RMLs and RCLs, has since become a common feature of many body designs, and can be seen on current low-floor double deckers in London.

Back at Park Royal, as time went on the build rate of Routemasters did fluctuate, but all succeeding orders to the first 850 perhaps inevitably went to the bodybuilder. Many of those working on them probably thought they had a job for life so the mid-1960s decision to end production came as a shock. It took longer than usual to complete the last few, owing to parts shortages. With a continuing production run it is easy to quietly replace an inadvertently damaged part by another one from the rack, and it is only at the very end that the shortage is discovered, and an extra one or two parts have to be ordered.

ER 882, as it was originally classified, stands outside the factory minus front grille and battery cover. The classification was changed to RML because LT management wanted the letters 'RM' included in the code and by 1961 it had been decided that the RML classification reserved for Leyland RMs would not be used.

Worthy of special mention are the interiors of the second batch of forward-entrance Routemasters built for Northern General. John Reid, a well-known design consultant, was responsible for the décor – and at about the same time also styled a unique batch of Park Royal-bodied Albion coaches. The 1960s had seen many operators trying to brighten up and generally modernise the interiors, but most soon dated. Reid's did not and also wore quite well. Ceilings were a beige plastic laminate with a doodles design of criss-cross lines, while side lining panels, seatbacks and front bulkhead were a brown version of the same doodles. Window surrounds were matt black. Moquette was a tartan design with light beige edgings and seat tops. The overall effect was light and modern yet practical.

As a journalist I made a number of visits to Park Royal, usually to see mainly its other production of the time, which included Bridgemasters for East Yorkshire with upper decks designed to fit through the Beverley Bar. My guide there was always D T Davies, whose title today would probably be contracts manager. It was he who produced detailed specifications from which materials would be ordered and which guided the workforce. After a chat about who might be buying what and why in the industry, there was usually a works tour. There would always be a Routemaster in build, either short or long, red, dark red, green or blue. Outside the buildings would be that strange array seen at no other bodybuilder: 'A' frames complete with engine, front wheels and steering wheel. Inside I always found the upholstery shop fascinating with its range of tasteful (and sometimes dreadful) moquettes. Seat cushions were attached to their plywood bases with tintacks: the upholsterers would grab a handful of tintacks, put them in their mouth, and then spit them out one by one as required on to the end of the special magnetic hammers they used. One other strange feature at Park Royal as time went on was the painting, still done by brush. The finish attained was superb. It was not until the early 1970s, long after Routemaster building had ended, that spray painting was introduced.

Park Royal Vehicles' yard in 1962. RMs are seen in the company of a Bridgemaster for East Yorkshire and a Regent V for East Kent.

Union Matters

Finally we look at the introduction of RMs to replace members of the RT family and the power of the trade union at that time to thwart London Transport's intention to carry out replacement using new schedules reflecting the higher capacity of the Routemaster.

At the beginning of the 1960s, shortages of drivers and conductors at London Transport were at an all-time high of 18%, even after the 10% cuts in services that followed the six-week bus strike of 1958. Not only had passengers been lost following the strike, many staff too had decided to move away from buses. A fairly substantial pay rise in 1960 helped to some extent, but London Transport now had to look for other ways in which to deal with what would clearly be a long-term problem. In 1961, London Transport began to talk to the trade union about what it had had in mind since 1953: replacing RTs with RMs on the basis of taking into account the higher seating capacity to reduce the number of buses and staff required.

Before these discussions, London Transport decided to order an experimental batch of twenty-four 30ft-long 72-seater Routemasters. On 8th March 1961 the Executive received confirmation that an order for these had been placed and that design details had been settled between the LT and AEC design offices. The extended Routemasters were first mentioned to the union on 20th March, when operating manager John Burnell brought up the subject at a meeting with union officials. The response of the union was that it could not take part in any experiment involving the operation of 72-seater buses in London. Burnell was treading carefully – even rather deceitfully – as he claimed that "there was a proposal in mind for the obtaining of 24 Routemasters of increased length" when the buses had in fact already been ordered. Indeed the drawings for the 30ft long version were completed at Chiswick just two days after the meeting.

On 10th April, at another meeting with the union, Mr Burnell told the union representative that "an order was being placed". The union rep reminded Mr Burnell of its position. Then, on 4th July, London Transport attempted to open up negotiations for the experimental operation of 30ft long buses in "inner central London" on routes then worked by RT buses. By 24th July one of the extended Routemasters was available for inspection and the operating manager invited union officials to view it. The union responded by saying that as they did not desire to participate in the experiment they would not wish to inspect the bus.

London Transport then decided that instead of using the 30ft long Routemasters on RT routes, twelve of them would be used in Stage 12 of the trolleybus conversion scheduled for 8th November, route 104 being selected during the first half of August. No decision had been made at this time in respect of the other twelve RMLs. Dennis Counihan, the traffic superintendent for Central Road Services, mentioned the intention at the end of a meeting with two union officials on 17th August. It was a fairly casual reference, which rather upset the union officials, one of whom wrote the same day to the new operating manager Fred Lloyd. The official complained about the manner in which the union had been informed and demanded the "immediate withdrawal" of the decision to use the 72-seater buses.

Fred Lloyd replied on 23rd August to the effect that he could see no justification for the complaint about the manner in which the union had been told, playing down the significance of the introduction of 72-seater buses by pointing out that they were replacing trolleybuses of the same length and seating 70 passengers. He asked the union to agree that it was a different matter from introducing larger buses on RT routes and said that the decision to use the buses on route 104 could not be altered. A concession was subsequently won by the union which meant that drivers and conductors of the RMLs at Finchley would have their time on duty reduced by 5%. Drivers already trained on RMs were each given one hour of training to handle the longer version and from 8th November the full allocation on route 104 (19 buses) was worked by RMLs.

Just over a week later, on 16th November, there was a meeting between London Transport and TGWU officials to discuss productivity and how staff might be rewarded for working larger buses elsewhere. The Executive wanted to discuss productivity allowances for the implementation of a five-point plan: (a) introduction of one-man bus operation on Central buses; (b) conversion of routes from RT to RM operation; (c) conversion to RML operation; (d) operation of standee buses; (e) increasing the maximum speed of schedules from 30mph to 40mph. A joint committee was set up of union representatives and officers from London Transport's bus operating, schedules, labour relations and finance departments. Two meetings followed between then and April 1962 and discussions centred on the replacement of RTs by RM or RML buses and the conversion of some Central bus RF routes to one-man operation.

The proposal put to the union in respect of the RM was that 10 RMs would replace 11 RTs and that the operating staff working the new buses would receive 40% of the financial savings. Theoretical schedules had been compiled which showed a 9½% reduction in the number of buses required on routes converted from RT to RM and an average 5% saving in staff requirements. This would go a long way towards reducing the staff shortage and therefore reducing unreliability. London Transport's intention was to introduce RMs in areas where it was difficult to recruit sufficient staff or where the passenger demand would be handled more efficiently with the larger bus. Some of the duties saved would enable the introduction of new services or route extensions (within the constraints of staff availability).

From the start, the union wanted productivity savings to be spread more widely than amongst the operating staff working on routes converted to RM after completion of the trolleybus conversion. A number of RT routes had already been converted to RM as part of the integration of former trolleybus services and the union felt that all of the RMs introduced since 1959 should be included in the deal. Another demand that came into the discussions was for part of the busmen's share of the savings to be given in the form of a reduction in working hours, thereby improving working conditions and making the job more attractive.

On 2nd July 1962, the union was informed the first area to be treated would be Harrow. Routes 114, 140 and 158 would be converted from RT to RM (on the 10 for 11 basis) and at the same time a new route 230A between Harrow Weald garage and Northwick Park station via Belmont would be introduced and there would be an extension of route 90B from Yeading to South Harrow to provide support for the 140 over this section. Seven buses would be saved by the conversion of routes 114, 140 and 158 and the two buses needed for the new 230A would be matched by a similar reduction in the number allocated to the 230. Two more buses would be needed for the 90B extension, but this route was operated from Twickenham garage where staff recruitment was less of a problem. The buses on the routes receiving RMs would be saved by reducing the frequencies in the peak hours (some quite severe reductions were also planned at weekends). The 114 for example would be reduced in the peaks from every five minutes to every six. Schemes for other areas would have followed a similar pattern.

Route 73, with a total scheduled allocation of 90 buses, also figured at an early stage and the proposal here was that it would receive 90 RMs in order to discover whether introducing RMs on a one-for-one basis, an increase in capacity of 14%, would result in an increase in passenger numbers. As negotiations dragged on with no sign of agreement, one option looked at was to convert some routes, without reducing schedules, at garages where drivers and maintenance staff were already trained for RMs. A complete list of such garages was drawn up from which routes 7 (Middle Row garage), 81/A/B (Hounslow) and 233 (Wood Green) were selected for possible conversion, using a total of 67 RMs. Added by hand to the typewritten list on which these routes appeared was a note that it would take about five weeks to train drivers for the 9 and 73 routes.

When RT family buses were used for stages 1–3 of the trolleybus conversion it was on the basis that these routes would be the first to be converted to RM when the replacement of trolleybuses had been completed. While the trolleybus conversion was in progress this idea was abandoned. By 1961 it had been decided that part of the batch of 1520 Routemasters that had been authorised in 1956 would be built as coaches and the first conversions to Routemaster after the completion of trolleybus replacement were of Green Line routes. A batch of 68 RMCs began to enter service on Green Line work on 29th August 1962 without, it seems, any resistance from the union despite frequency reductions being made to reflect the higher seating capacity. Country bus staff tended to accept changes much more readily than their Central bus colleagues.

The RMs that entered service in December and January 1962/63 had a baptism of snow in particularly severe January weather which showed up some anti-freeze problems. Rye Lane's RM 1383 is seen at Grove Park station.

One of the sticking points in the negotiations was the demand by the union that the 6,000 staff already working Routemasters on the former trolleybus routes should share the productivity savings. London Transport had resisted this since negotiations had started in November 1961, but in July 1962 when a settlement was becoming urgent, the inclusion of the ex-trolleybus men in the deal was conceded subject to the five-point productivity package being accepted.

The union rejected this package shortly after it was presented to them and there followed nine more meetings with London Transport between August and November. In early October, in order to gain acceptance for the RM conversion of routes 114, 140 and 158, the percentage share of the savings offered was increased from 40% to 42½%. The conversion, scheduled for 10th October, failed to go ahead for lack of agreement and on 19th October the offer was increased to 45%.

Ten days later the union responded with what it called a compromise proposal in respect of the method of sharing out the offer. The busmen remained resistant to cuts in the number of drivers and conductors and this was the fundamental difference between them and London Transport that prevented an agreement being reached. London Transport wanted to reduce the requirement for staff to match the staff available, whereas the busmen wanted working conditions and pay improved to attract the staff needed. Under London Transport's plans 5% fewer bus operating staff would have been needed when the changeover was complete.

Discussions with the union in October and November 1962 suggest that Dalston would have been the next garage to receive RMs after Harrow Weald and route 73, involving routes 9, 11 and 47. Route 9 was shared with Mortlake, whose only other route was the 73, and route 11 was shared with Riverside. Route 47 was shared with Bromley and Catford. On the basis of Routemasters being used to reduce the number of buses and crew duties, west and north-west London would have been among the priorities as garages here had some of the worst staff shortages of the network, but there was also the need to spread the new buses around or south and south-east London, where staff was easier to get, would have hardly any Routemasters in the early years of the changeover. Operating staff requirements at Dalston would have reduced by 4½% from 214 to 204 if RMs had been introduced in this way.

At a meeting on 2nd November to discuss a union compromise proposal of 29th October, it became clear that the negotiations that had been going on for very nearly a year were not going to result in a settlement. The union was by now asking for the existing Country Bus one-man operations to be included in the productivity package and for garage maintenance staff to receive a share. As London Transport had made it clear that 45% was the maximum share of cost savings it was prepared to pass on to the staff, the individual payments would be very small if spread so widely. A joint delegate conference of the union had already voted by 74 votes to 34 against accepting the offer on the table, which included a 3% reduction in the maximum scheduled time on duty each day, despite the negotiators recommending acceptance. With little further movement, the negotiating committee saw no point in recommending it a second time. The productivity allowance scheme was therefore withdrawn by London Transport and the decision taken to proceed with the introduction of RMs without alteration to Monday to Friday schedules.

By now around 200 RMs were waiting to go into service and further buses were arriving at the rate of seven per week. Plans were urgently drawn up to use the RMs on some of the busiest routes where their extra capacity would be of most benefit. It was announced on 19th November that the first routes to receive them would be, in order of conversion, the 73, 37, 13, 16, 36, 36A and 36B and that driver training would start within days. On 12th December over 120 new RMs were allocated to Tottenham, Mortlake, Stockwell and Putney garages for use on routes 73 and 37 and by the beginning of 1963 over 200 RMs had taken over from RT family buses.

A matter of common concern between management and union was that of the increased rate of accidents with the RM compared with trolleybuses or RTs. It had been suggested that a cause may have been the inability of the driver to see the nearside wing and, as an experiment, 25 RMs at West Ham and Highgate garages were fitted with width gauges in 1961. Further investigations showed that in the majority of cases, accident damage was to the offside of the RMs. This coupled with Durrant's concerns about the gauges' vulnerability to vandalism, led to no further buses being fitted with them and the 25 experimental ones being removed. A later review of the training of new drivers found that drivers who had been trained on RT or RTL buses had a tendency to underestimate the speed of the RM owing to the comparative lightness of the controls and its easier manoeuvrability. Inadequate control had often been found in the approach to corners and in recovery of steering. The power assisted steering, the report continued, allowed the bus to draw out too sharply from stops, and was often used to swing the front of the bus out without due consideration for other road users. Additionally it was pointed out that the engine was less efficient as a brake than on the RT types, with a consequent need for the driver to make an earlier decision when it was necessary to adjust the speed of the bus. The report, dated February 1963, also raised the matter of the width of the RM and the lack of vision of the nearside wing, but on this matter nothing further was done.

In the same month, at a meeting of the Bus Allocation Advisory Committee, the trade union raised the matter of RT and RTL buses working on RM routes and the fact that drivers often had to work part of their duty on an RM and part on an RT/RTL. The driver could be faced with the difficulty, the union representative said, of operating a bus with automatic gearbox and left-hand handbrake at the start of his duty and then needing to switch to a bus with manual gearbox and right-hand handbrake. It was pointed out by the management that the long-established method of cross-linking buses in the peaks – i.e. a bus operating on one route in the morning peak and another in the evening – made this inevitable. In addition the policy was to have a predominance of RT/RTL spares over RM spares to avoid spare RMs getting out on routes they were not suitable for.

One of the width gauges fitted to 25 RMs to see if they would reduce the number of accidents.

At the height of the productivity negotiations, London Transport took delivery of RMF 1254. An experiment with such a vehicle had first been discussed by London Transport management in October 1961. Fred Lloyd referred to a deteriorating trend of uncollected fares. He felt that a vehicle with a front entrance and doors under the control of the driver would give relief to the conductor, who could then concentrate fully on collecting the fares. Durrant reported to Lloyd on 23rd November 1961 that work was in hand with Park Royal Vehicles to design front entrance versions of both the RM and the RML.

At the Central Road Services committee meeting of 21st February 1962 Fred Lloyd told those present that he was going ahead, as an experiment, with the production of one front entrance Routemaster, though whether it would be an RM or an RML had not yet been decided. By the beginning of March, however, the decision had been made in favour of a 30ft long vehicle. At a Road Services meeting on 1st March the possibility of operating a bus with front entrance and rear exit was discussed so that passengers could board and alight simultaneously. The driver would be responsible for operating both sets of doors but would have sight of the rear platform and doors only through a mirror. This idea was not pursued.

Some interest in the RMF came from outside London also as both AEC and Park Royal had hoped. On 13th July the Director and General Manager of Park Royal Vehicles Ltd, J W Shirley, wrote to Fred Lloyd to say that Liverpool Corporation had indicated interest and Shirley asked if London Transport would be willing to let them operate it for a period not exceeding four weeks. Lloyd agreed that they could have the bus for four weeks, without charge except the cost of collection and return to London. The bus would retain full London Transport livery throughout. He went on to say that London Transport would wish to use the vehicle for a month following the Commercial Motor Show, and Liverpool could borrow it afterwards. It was decided at a Road Services meeting on 19th July that the bus would be allocated for the first month of trial use in London to route 104. Michael Robbins, by now a member of the Executive, said that he thought it essential that at some point the RMF should be tried out on a busy route in central London. Lloyd still wanted to have a 27ft 6ins long RMF built as well, but the Executive insisted that experience first be gained with RMF 1254.

Such experience was not to be had, but as late as 14th September – just before the bus was exhibited at Earls Court – the Operational Research Team set up to monitor RMF 1254 made plans for their work, apparently oblivious to potential problems with the staff. The team's terms of reference were "to assess the effect in operation of the RMF bus compared with the RML vehicles already operating on route 104, with special reference to the effects on running time and on time at stops, the work of the crew and on uncollected fares". The team was advised that Monday 8th October was the tentative date for entry into service. This was just two days before new RMs were due to enter service at Harrow Weald and London Transport and the union were still without agreement. It should therefore have been no surprise that the response from the busmen was that they were not prepared to operate RMF 1254 until the productivity package had been agreed. In addition, a letter from Fred Lloyd to his assistant M J McCoy dated 15th August indicates that there was still some ill-feeling at Finchley. Lloyd had spoken about the RMLs to the men there, who felt that "the method of putting them in was perhaps sharp practice on our part".

When the RMLs began to enter Central Area service in quantity in 1965, these were also introduced on a one-for-one basis, giving some routes that had progressed from RT to RM and then to RML a total increase in capacity of 28½%. The 70-seater bus ideas of 1939 and 1949 had arrived (plus two seats) but without the savings in buses of up to 22% envisaged in 1949. By 1965 LT had decided that the search for productivity lay in large-scale one-man operation and no further orders for Routemasters were placed beyond RML 2760. Another idea from 1949, the standee single decker – this time minus the conductor – was revived as part of the plan for one-manning.

The amount of money spent on the RM in development and during its early years of troublesome running, coupled with the failure to reach a productivity agreement based on its increased capacity, mean that if each RM had had a service life of 18 years as designed, the model would have been far from a success. That circumstances led to some of the type lasting at least three times longer to become an icon of London was a fortunate redemption.

Tailpiece

This is not a genuine photograph but a computer generated image by Tim Demuth that gives an impression of a full-width cab version of the RM based on the first mock-up. Douglas Scott recalled doing some sketches of a full-front design which he did not keep. At no time was London Transport keen on a full-width cab for the new bus and no mock-up or model was actually produced. Design is to a large extent a matter of taste, but the first half-cab design by Scott, as shown on the front cover, was arguably the most attractive of any of the designs either proposed or used.

Sources

Transport for London's Archive and Record Management Service

The following files were consulted

LT000232/284
LT000264/128
LT000115/179
LT000315/408
A0343/005
LT000366/001–004
LT000367/87
LN214/2/LT000233/338
LT00011S/209/A0153/042
S94-059
LT26 OM(CRS)
LT106 OM(CRS)
LN377 OM(CRS)
LN377 OM(CB)
LT000022

Trade Journals

Bus & Coach 1950, 1953, 1954
The Commercial Motor September and October 1954
Motor Transport September and October 1954
Passenger Transport 22nd September 1954

Photographs supplied by

Colin Curtis, Tony Packer, Alan A Townsin, London's Transport Museum, John Aldridge, Fred Ivey, Michael Dryhurst, Alan B Cross, Andrew Morgan, Peter Relf, Mick Webber.

The drawings from *Passenger Transport* and *Buses Illustrated* (on pages 36 and 41) are reproduced by permission of Ian Allan Ltd.

The photographs on pages 16 and 17 were retouched by Lucy Day. The photographs on the cover and on pages 2, 38 and 62 (right) are black and white originals coloured by Tim Demuth.